Presented to:

_____

From:

_____

with Dr. David Jeremiah

Edited by William Kruidenier

Unless otherwise indicated, Scripture verses quoted are from the
NEW KING JAMES VERSION.

Printed in the United States of America.

Answers to Questions About
ADVERSITY

DAVID JEREMIAH

Table of Contents

Unanswered Questions   61

Christian Living   141

INTRODUCTION

Since we have a limited number of days on earth, it seems a shame to spend so many of them in pain, sickness, suffering, temptation, and trouble. With so few days allotted to us, why are some spent in hospitals and foxholes? Like the weather, some of our days are fair; others are fairly awful. Why, we wonder, is life so hard?

This question has haunted humanity from the beginning. The greatest thinkers of the ages have wrestled with this—and not just writers like Job, Sartre, and Descartes. Today's pop pundits grapple with suffering in almost every movie and novel that comes along. Screenwriter Woody Allen summed it up, saying, "Life is full of misery, loneliness, and suffering—and it's all over much too soon."[1]

I'd probably feel that way too if I didn't have the encouragement of Scripture. Like you, I've faced sorrow, sickness, and scary days. I can't complain; I've enjoyed a blessed life. But I've also had painful bends in the road and periods when I've wondered, "What in the world is going on?"

I don't have all the answers, but God understands everything better than we do. He resides in His holy temple and reigns on His heavenly throne. He took all the suffering in the world, boiled it down to its evil essence, shaped it into the form of a cross, and sent Jesus to take care of it. It took six hours. But in the shadow of Calvary an eternal answer arrived to the problem of pain. Because Jesus faced adversity, He defeated the Adversary. Because He defeated the Adversary, we can trust Him with adversities in life. His grace is sufficient.

There are promises in God's Word to meet all our needs, to give us peace amid the problems and strength for every struggle. God has answers to your questions about adversity. I pray that in the following pages you'll find insights from His Word to encourage you on your journey—whether today finds you in sunshine or storm.

1. Quoted by Elisabeth Wilson in *Stress Proof Your Life* (Oxford: The Infinite Ideas Company Limited, 2005), 87.

ADVERSITY

Many *are* the
afflictions of the
righteous, but the
LORD delivers him
out of them all.

Psalm 34:19

PAIN AND SUFFERING

Why does God allow pain?

The Word of God is brutally honest about the reality of life. Sometimes in the process of growing up in God's family, we feel the sting of adversity. It doesn't feel good, and we would not really desire it. But God has a purpose in our pain that we may not see or understand in the present. We can trust that our pain is no secret to Him. Everything that happens to us will become a platform for the glory of Him who "works all things according to the counsel of His will" (Ephesians 1:11). God uses problems in our lives to drive us to Him as our only hope, our only source of dependence. Difficulty is often one phase of divine discipline (meaning training toward maturity). It is unfortunate that many teachers today say that if we love God and we walk with Him, we will never be sick, we will never suffer, we will never know poverty or financial hardship—we will never experience any of that! That doctrine is not from the Word of God! Jesus Himself said, "These things I have spoken to you, that in Me you may have peace. In the world you will have tribulation; but be of good cheer, I have overcome the world" (John 16:33).

Whether Jesus calms the storm around you or calms you in the midst of the storm, you're safe wherever He is.

If I'm following the Lord, shouldn't I be exempt from adversity?

Adversity is no respecter of persons. I've been in a few "perfect storms" in my life and during those times, I have never felt those struggles happened because I was out of the will of God. Indeed, just the opposite. Sometimes we experience perfect storms not because we have disobeyed God but because we have obeyed Him. God Himself allows us to experience difficult times and sudden trouble not because we've done anything wrong, but because we may be doing something right. Jesus always did the right thing, yet "He learned obedience by the things which He suffered" (Hebrews 5:8).

The most important lessons I've learned in my life have been learned in times of challenge. God uses critics and enemies and problems and dangers to drive us to Himself. The key is to trust less in self and more in God, and one of the ways we learn this lesson is through adversity.

Few of us ever fully grasp this simple but painful truth: The heat of suffering is a refiner's fire, purifying the gold of godly character and wisdom.

Can anything good come from my pain?

The Bible says not to be discouraged when you have a disruptive moment. That is often a difficult truth to embrace in the midst of a painful event. God's Word assures us, though, that problems and pain can be like a teacher in our life, instructing us in the ways of maturity. For our suffering "yields the peaceable fruit of righteousness to those who have been trained by it" (Hebrews 12:11). Pain can be our teacher!

Even as we confront illness, pain, and injury, we need to be biblical Christians claiming God's promises and living with His presence and purposes in mind. When experiencing adversity, it helps to remember that the biblical heroes of old weren't immunized against pain in life; Scripture is filled with accounts of their suffering. Job lived a life of integrity, and yet he lost his family, his wealth, the admiration of his wife, and his health. Peter's mother-in-law occupied a sickbed. Samuel became feeble. King David anguished over the condition of his newborn son. Every biblical character called by God experienced problems in life—so pain is not exclusive to us.

Even the Son of Man suffered violent, life-ending injuries and excruciating pain at the hands of His enemies in order to carry out God's will for His life (Philippians 2:8-10).

When we encounter pain, the question should not be, *Why is this happening to me?* or, *What am I going to do?* Instead, we should pray, *Lord, what do you want to teach me in this disruptive moment? I am Your ready and willing student—teach me everything You know I need. I don't want to waste this suffering. I want to walk through it and come out on the other side having learned everything I can so that it will be an occasion for God to be glorified.*

God allows no pain without purpose.

Should I reveal the pain I am feeling to others?

Besides preaching, a fair amount of posturing takes place on Sunday mornings—meaning, we sometimes work hard at dressing up our problems so no one will know the true state of our soul. Sometimes it's a matter of logistics. People who attend only a worship service have little opportunity to talk about how they are really doing in life. But even in small groups, where transparency is encouraged, sometimes people lack courage. It takes time to cultivate a culture of courage that will allow individuals to pull back the curtain on their life.

The Bible encourages us to "bear one another's burdens, and so fulfill the law of Christ" (Galatians 6:2). And there are two sides to that coin of caring: being a burden sharer and a burden bearer. Each of us can share our burdens *with* others as well as bear the burdens *of* others. In both cases—sharing and bearing—the rule is the same: with "a spirit of gentleness" (Galatians 6:1), "speaking the truth in love" (Ephesians 4:15).

Do all Christians endure suffering at some point in their lives?

The Bible teaches that, because we live in a fallen world, we can expect to experience pain, suffering, or disruptive events in life. The three friends of Job weren't right about everything, but they were right about trouble: "Yet man is born to trouble, as the sparks fly upward" (Job 5:7). Beyond "general" troubles in life, followers of Christ are told to expect that their allegiance to Him will be the cause of even more pointed pain (2 Timothy 3:12). Peter wrote that we shouldn't be surprised when we suffer as Christians (1 Peter 4:12-16).

You may wonder, *What is the purpose of pain in the Christian's life?* Ultimately, it is so we might become like Christ by living in total dependence on, and perfect obedience to, God. That was the relationship the first Adam (and Eve) had with God, and Christ came as "the last Adam" (1 Corinthians 15:45) to restore it. But change can be painful; every painful experience in life causes us to choose to depend upon our own resources or to depend on God. As we see the fruit of dependence on God, we learn to trust Him more and ourselves less. The apostle Paul said of his own painful experience, "Therefore most gladly I will rather boast in my infirmities, that the power of Christ may rest upon me. . . . For when I am weak [in myself], then I am strong [in Christ]" (2 Corinthians 12:9b-10).

Suffering as a Christian has another purpose: It helps us identify with the sufferings of Christ and grow in anticipation and joy at the thought of seeing Him when He returns (Romans 8:17). As we identify with the suffering of Christ through painful experiences, the life of Christ can be revealed through us. "Therefore let those who suffer according to the will of God commit their souls *to Him* in doing good, as to a faithful Creator" (1 Peter 4:19).

> *Even in life's most difficult moments, God's love is sufficient.*

Should I prepare for suffering in my life?

As followers of Christ we should be prepared to experience what He experienced: great joy as well as times of trouble. That is the reality of life in this world, and it is no different for Christians. The apostle Paul acknowledged both realities when he wrote that we should "rejoice with those who rejoice, and weep with those who weep" (Romans 12:15).

A wise and maturing Christian should prepare himself for what he knows will likely come in life—and that includes troubling circumstances. Just as a soldier puts on his armor *before* the battle in order to be ready for the conflict, so the Christian should clothe himself in the armor of God as a defense against not only the attacks of Satan but other disruptive events of life (Ephesians 6:10-18). Central to that armor is the sword of the Spirit, the Word of God. In Scripture we have "exceedingly great and precious promises" that *"pertain* to life and godliness" (2 Peter 1:3-4). The more knowledge we have of God and His ways, the more likely will we be able to stand firm against the storms of life (Matthew 7:24-25). Studying, memorizing, praying over, and meditating on God's Word will keep trouble from surprising us—either as to the cause of trouble or how to manage it. The Bible cannot make trouble disappear, but it can give us assurance that it is transitory and "not worthy *to be compared* with the glory which shall be revealed in us" (Romans 8:18).

It is not the absence of suffering but the response to suffering that makes Christians unique.

How can I get past the discouragement of a personal disaster?

The prophet Jeremiah warned of the coming destruction of Jerusalem; but when the end came in 586 B.C., he was still filled with sorrow and his spirit was broken. We can relate to how he felt. Jeremiah took the attack upon his city very personally, like it had happened to him and him alone. In the midst of all of the carnage of Jerusalem, Jeremiah paused for a moment in his grieving, and he took time to remember God's faithfulness—and what he recalled restored a sense of hope to his soul.

Our world today is facing destruction as well. Our hearts are often troubled by terrorism, disease and public health issues, financial crises, catastrophic weather events, and more. Like Jeremiah, there has to come a moment when we stop and remember the Word of our Lord. If we are going to make the journey from discouragement and despair to hope, we must fill our hearts with compassion and find our strength in God. Regardless of events going on around us, we need to faithfully continue serving Him. As we build our lives on the rock foundation of Jesus Christ, we can use our resources and influence to extend His kingdom—making a contribution that will outlive us and outlast us, and restore hope for the future.

Discouragement is life's invitation for you to start living supernaturally once again.

How can I remain calm in the midst of chaos?

It's easy to forget that first century Israel—especially Jerusalem—was not a particularly peaceful place to live. The iron boot of Rome moved swiftly to keep its version of the peace, and there was a constant undercurrent of religious tensions. Throw in poverty, famine, diseases, wars—there was plenty to keep the heart unsettled (as there is in our day). So it comes as no surprise to read what Jesus said to His disciples: "Peace I leave with you, My peace I give to you; not as the world gives do I give to you. Let not your heart be troubled, neither let it be afraid" (John 14:27).

Jesus spoke those words on the night of His betrayal and arrest. In addition to everyday disruptions, He knew what the coming events would do to His disciples' faith and peace of mind. They would be confused about His death and would face certain persecution after His resurrection and ascension. Jesus wanted His disciples not to seek peace in their surroundings and circumstances but in Him. Jesus knew exactly what was coming in His life, His disciples' lives, and He knows what is coming in ours. He wants us to find our peace in Him.

Even though it may look for a moment like everything is wrong with our world, we can have a security, and a peace, and a confidence that comes with knowing that the One to whom we go in prayer is in control. Regardless of the situation we may find ourselves in—our heart and mind are guarded by "the peace of God, which surpasses all understanding." He is our peace in the time of storm.

> **And the LORD, He *is* the One who goes before you. He will be with you, He will not leave you nor forsake you; do not fear nor be dismayed.**
>
> *Deuteronomy 31:8*

FACING FEARS AND FAILURE

How can I face my fears?

When you find yourself in the cave of fear and discouragement, when anxiety descends upon your life, the first thing you need to do is to acknowledge the reliability of your God. He is in charge! Nothing that is happening in your life has caught Him by surprise. When you begin to be fearful, immediately turn your attention away from your fear and toward the face of Almighty God.

Before David became king of Israel, he feared for his life by the hand of the existing king, Saul. On one occasion, he hid in a cave with his supporters (1 Samuel 22:1-2). While there, he poured out his heart to God: "I cry out to the Lord with my voice; with my voice to the Lord I make my supplication. I pour out my complaint before Him; I declare before Him my trouble" (Psalm 142:1). He acknowledged his fear to God.

When Christians face their fears they must also acknowledge the reliability of God, the adequacy of God as our defense against fear. It helps us to confess that God knows all our needs, that nothing takes Him by surprise, and that He is able to provide the resources that we lack: "Be merciful to me, O God, be merciful to me! For my soul trusts in You; and in the shadow of Your wings I will make my refuge, until *these* calamities have passed by. I will cry out to God Most High, to God who performs *all things* for me" (Psalm 57:1-2). Focusing on God instead of on fear elevates Him to His proper place in our heart and mind.

> *Face your fear with this assurance: "perfect love casts out fear"*
> ~ 1 John 4:18

Why is it so crucial not to worry?

As a wise person has said, "Worry is like enjoying a rocking chair. It burns up calories, but it doesn't get you anywhere." To worry is to expend energy without changing anything. The New Testament word for *worry* is translated by the phrase "to take thought" or "to be careful." It comes from a Greek word which means "to have a divided mind." To worry is to have part of the mind focused on the present and part focused on the future. But worrying can neither change nor control the future. It is inconsistent for you to worry once you recognize that everything you have comes from God. Three times in Matthew 6:25-34, Jesus said, "Do not worry," and He went on to explain why: "Who of you by worrying can add a single hour to his life?" (verse 28) Worry and anxiety change nothing except the worrier—and it is always in negative ways. Instead of worrying about a future you can't change, put your faith in the One to whom the future belongs.

What does it mean to "wait on the Lord"? I am impatient for an answer.

"Waiting on the Lord" means God is at work, but He works on His timetable and feels no obligation to coincide His timetable with yours or mine. We may say, "God, would you please resolve this?" And He says, "Yes." "Would you please resolve this now?" And He says, "Wait." And we don't like to wait. Part of the problem is how we define waiting. Biblical waiting is not passive inactivity; it is not sitting around, twiddling our thumbs. Instead, waiting is active—it is walking in step with God as He invites us to journey with Him in the unfolding of His plans.

In the waiting, we learn; in the waiting, we grow. Waiting is what happens between the promise and the fulfillment. Waiting builds our faith. Waiting reminds us that God does not live on our schedule; we live on His. And if we will learn to wait, we will see God do some great things. Waiting is what God sometimes uses to help us see His will more clearly, to embrace it more joyfully when it is made fully clear. One benefit of waiting on God is often revealed only with time—we look back and see how God was working things out all along. Just because we can't *see* God at work doesn't mean He *isn't* at work. God is always working out His will whether He tells us or not. The psalmist has it right: "Rest in the LORD, and wait patiently for Him" (Psalm 37:7). In waiting, we learn to build our trust in God.

God sees all the doors and windows of opportunity—He knows when to close and open them at the perfect time.

How do I remain strong when facing an ongoing illness?

The greatest challenge in the loss of health is to keep trusting God. We know that He cares for us and that we have ultimate healing through the shed blood and empty tomb of Jesus Christ. But the loss of health affects us emotionally as much as physically. It puts us at risk financially and vocationally. It sets us on a collision course with our most dreaded enemy—death—and we may find ourselves in real mortal danger, exposed to possible suffering, chronic pain, and the loss of all we hold dear in life.

When our car breaks down, we take advantage of those who have repair skills. In the much more important area of our health, we do the same. We pray for God to guide us to doctors who can help; we pray for their wisdom and skill; we discipline ourselves to follow healing regimens; we trust God to do "exceedingly abundantly above all that we ask or think"(Ephesians 3:20). Health challenges should be faced the same way we face any other challenge in the Christian life—with faith in God's power to accomplish His purposes.

It is important to remember that as long as we're in this world, God intends to use us. Our work isn't over until He takes us home. Christian history tells us that some of the greatest works for God have been done by people battling illness or disability. Illness is many things, not the least of which is the opportunity to grow deeper in Christ. Many, including myself, can attest to the spiritual growth that can occur during health challenges. Priorities become clearer than ever before. The promises of God are read with refined eyes. And spiritually, we grow grateful for the grace of God and the gift of life.

In sickness or health, we should persevere—to do the work God has for us each day. If heaven is the worst thing that can happen to us, we shouldn't despair even amid medical emergencies or the loss of health. We have a Great Physician whose own tomb is empty. We have a heavenly home prepared for us. And we have a sympathetic Savior who never imparts a spirit of fear, but of power, love, and a sound mind (2 Timothy 1:7). Cast all your cares on Him, knowing He cares for you (1 Peter 5:7).

> **What happens when a person dies? I am fearful of dying.**

The Bible speaks of physical death and spiritual death. When a person dies physically, the soul and spirit leave the body in an inanimate state on earth. Those who die physically in Christ are united spiritually with God, while those who die apart from Christ await the final judgment. Physical death, therefore, is the separation of the soul and spirit from the body.

Spiritual death is the separation of the soul and spirit from God. It is possible to be physically alive on earth while being spiritually dead. Paul describes those "who were dead in trespasses and sins" in Ephesians 2:1. Paul also wrote that sin entered the world through Adam and spread to every person (Romans 5:12), and that the "wages of sin is death" (Romans 6:23). Spiritually dead persons are "made alive" through faith in Christ (Ephesians 2:1). Whatever one's spiritual condition at the time of physical death—whether spiritually alive or spiritually dead—passes through to eternity.

So physical death is the separation of the spiritual nature of man from the body, while spiritual death is the separation of the spiritual nature of man from God. For a Christian, physical death is nothing more than a doorway through which we pass into eternal life. Jesus said it best: "I am the resurrection and the life. He who believes in Me, though he may die, he shall live. And whoever lives and believes in Me shall never die" (John 11:25-26). There is no reason for a Christian to fear physical death. Through faith in Christ, we have eternal life even before we die physically (John 17:3).

For a Christian, physical death is nothing more than a doorway through which we pass into eternal life.

> **How will my soul travel to heaven when I die? The uncertainty causes me concern.**

This is a mystery to some, but even in our death, God has made provision for us. When I was young and someone died, at the visitation this phrase was often heard: "The angels came and took her." I didn't realize it then, but that is exactly what happens! When any of us who are believers pass from this life to the next, Almighty God dispatches angels to convey us into His presence. Jesus told a story about the deaths of a rich man and a poor man (Luke 16:19-31). When the poor man died, Jesus said, he "was carried by the angels to [heaven]" (verse 22). This is the only glimpse behind the curtain of death in the New Testament that gives us an image of how a Christian's spirit gets to heaven when he dies—angels come to earth to escort him there. We won't simply be beamed up to heaven; we will be carried there by the angels. On the day when you wait for the curtains to be drawn on this life, God's messengers will stand ready to bear you away on life's ultimate journey.

I spend a fair amount of time in airplanes traveling very fast and very high above the earth. But I know my spiritual transition from earth to heaven will make those trips pale in comparison. Escorted by angels, I will make the trip I have waited most of my life to take. It is a moment of which every Christian should live in joyful anticipation!

> *On the day when you wait for the curtains to be drawn on this life, God's messengers will stand ready to bear you away on life's ultimate journey.*

I am afraid to fail. How can I be effective for God?

Throughout Scripture, we see God reaching out to help His children overcome their fears and weaknesses. And nowhere is God's concern for His fearful servant more evident than in the way that He prepared Joshua to lead the children of Israel after the death of Moses. First of all, God promised Joshua, "As I was with Moses, *so* I will be with you" (Joshua 1:5). If you know that God is with you, you're already off to a good start. And then God assured Joshua of His purpose: "Now therefore, arise, go over this Jordan, you and all this people, to the land which I am giving to them—the children of Israel." And "every place that the sole of your foot will tread upon I have given you, as I said to Moses" (Joshua 1:2-3).

What God was doing for Joshua in this moment, and what He loves to do for us, was giving him focus. When you have focus in your life, your fears begin to subside. And since fear is the father of failure, as our fears diminish, there is less failure. When you don't know what to do and you're caught up in the ambivalence of an undirected life, fear comes in and begins to just take control. But when you get up every day with the knowledge that God has called you to something, and you know what it is, and you begin to focus your attention on it—your fear of failure is replaced with optimism and hope. There are no guarantees in Scripture that we will never fail, and experience tells us we will. Like an infant learning to walk, we run the risk of falling (failing) as we take steps of faith, but failure can be the stepping stone to success if we learn from it.

God has given us the ability to do things we may feel inadequate to accomplish, but with our eyes focused on Him, we can be courageous—ready to tackle the opportunities He places in our pathway. There is only one thing required of Christ's followers, and it is neither success nor perfection. It is faithfulness (1 Corinthians 4:2).

If God has given me a task, how can I be assured that I won't fail?

The Bible promises us some things—forgiveness, salvation, eternal life—but absolute success in all of life's endeavors isn't one of them, unless you define success the way God does—as being faithful (Matthew 25:21, 23). By that definition, we can always succeed if we are always faithful.

This we know: "He who calls you *is* faithful, who also will do *it*" (1 Thessalonians 5:24). "It" in that verse refers to our safe passage until we meet the Lord at His Second Coming. But it serves as a metaphor for much else: God does not call us without equipping us. If God has called you to a task—the Christian life, marriage, parenthood, ministry, vocation, or any other—you can rest assured that you will have what it takes to see it through. That makes the question not "Will I succeed?" but "Has God called me to do this?" The only way we can fail at such an endeavor is by doing it in our own strength and by our own will. We could even succeed in the eyes of the world yet fail in the eyes of God by not depending on Him. But there is no failure in God's eyes when we are obedient, faithful, trusting, and persevering in our commitment to Him.

God does not call us without equipping us.

How can I turn my failures into successes?

Every time we fail to reach a goal, we have the opportunity to try again. What a foolish thing it is to fail and not learn something. If we accept failure as the final and absolute judgment of our potential, then we are going to fail the rest of our lives. We have to learn to use failure as a resource, as an opportunity, and often it can be the door to great success.

John Keats, an English author, once wrote, "Failure is, in a sense, the highway to success, inasmuch as every discovery of what is false leads us to seek earnestly after what is true, and every fresh experience points out some form of error which we shall afterward carefully avoid."

If we study our failures, we'll see what we're doing wrong so we can find out how to do it right. Don't throw your failures away. Use them to help you succeed. If you are going in the same direction and falling in the same pitfall, then learn to go a different way. God often allows our failures to become distinctive points of power and ministry in our lives.

Is it possible to start fresh after I've failed deeply?

It is important to remember that the two most important people in the first century of the Church's expansion were two of its biggest "failures": the apostles Peter and Paul. Peter's failure to identify as a follower of Christ caused him great grief and shame (Matthew 26:75). Paul's failure to recognize Jesus as the Jewish Messiah, and his persecution of those who did believe, caused him later to refer to himself as the "chief" of sinners (1 Timothy 1:15). It's conceivable, humanly speaking, that both these men could have slunk into the shadows and never allowed God to use them. Yes, they would have accepted God's forgiveness, salvation, and restoration, but they might have sat in the back row of the Church for the rest of their lives. Instead, they processed their human failings and decided to take God at His Word and fulfill the missions given to them: Paul as apostle to the Gentiles and Peter as apostle to the Jews.

These men demonstrate what we all need to learn: failure is a *fact* of life, not a *way* of life. The fact of failure can be replaced by the fact of success through a series of choices we make. We make sure our relationships with God and other people are as they should be, we assess the appropriate ways to begin again, and we go forward. We must acknowledge that some failures take more time to correct and rebound from than others. But we start the process immediately—even if that process is repentance, restoration, restitution, reassessing, or redirection. We act as if we already know the answer to the question, Is there life after failure?—Yes! With God, all things are possible (Mark 9:23).

Only the Lord can turn our spiritual scars into trophies of His grace.

How can I fight feeling insecure with all that is going on in the world today?

When feeling insecure, the book of Psalms is a wonderful resource for anyone needing guidance, comfort, or help. An incredible portion of Scripture to offer comfort and direction during those times is the thirty-seventh Psalm.

Psalm 37 gives six steps for overcoming insecurity—written by a man who looked around and saw values and justice turned upside down in his day. *Step 1* is to "trust in the LORD" (verse 3). Trust God, not man. *Step 2,* "do good" (verse 3). Regardless of what others are doing, we are to do what God expects us to do. *Step 3* is to "dwell in the land, and feed on His faithfulness" (verse 3). If we are continually thankful for what God has done in our life and His faithfulness, our security will be in Him. *Step 4*—"Delight yourself also in the LORD" (verse 4). When our delight is in God, we gain His perspective on life. *Step 5:* "Commit your way to the LORD" (verse 5). When we are committed to God and His purposes, we will not fear the future. Finally, *Step 6* is to "rest in the LORD, and wait patiently for Him; do not fret because of him who prospers in his way" (verse 7). We are not to bear ill will toward those who seem prosperous in spite of ignoring God. We are to rest in God and wait for Him to settle up the accounts of justice, fairness, and righteousness.

Jesus offered this invitation to the weary and insecure: "Come to Me, all *you* who labor and are heavy laden, and I will give you rest" (Matthew 11:28). He is Lord over all. We can rest securely in Him.

> *Life's road is wide open to new places, opportunities, accomplishments, and amazing possibilities when God is in the driver's seat.*

How can I live for Jesus when everything around me seems to be disintegrating?

As the world breaks down, we can be built up! We are able to live for Jesus because we know what the "good and acceptable and perfect will of God" is. The more familiar we are with God's standards, the easier it is to see the world's ways by contrast— and do the opposite. The Bible says that if we're going to make it through this confusing time, we have to prevent the outward shape of our life from being fashioned like the world by taking care that our inward spirit is transformed regularly by the renewing of our minds. "And do not be conformed to this world, but be transformed by the renewing of your mind, that you may prove what *is* that good and acceptable and perfect will of God" (Romans 12:2). The British Bible translator J. B. Phillips gave us a memorable rendering of "do not be conformed . . . ." He wrote, "Don't let the world around you squeeze you into its own mould, but let God re-mould your minds from within." How do we renew, or "re-mould," our mind? By filling our mind with the Word of God.

The Christian benefits from a paradox: While the world is falling apart, he is being built up. While the kingdom of this world is disintegrating, the Christian is integrating himself into the kingdom of God. While the world is devolving into chaos and immaturity, we are evolving into order and maturity. While the world is passing away, the Christian is passing through on his way to heaven.

The world may seem to be disintegrating around you, but remember that God is still in control—renew your mind in Him.

UNANSWERED
QUESTIONS

Beloved, do not think it strange concerning the fiery trial which is to try you, as though some strange thing happened to you; but rejoice to the extent that you partake of Christ's sufferings, that when His glory is revealed, you may also be glad with exceeding joy.

1 Peter 4:12-13

GOD'S ANSWERS

> **What should I do if God's answer doesn't make sense to me?**

Sometimes life can seem like a swamp in the dead of night—the swamp of imponderables, full of things we don't understand. Even when we pray, and God answers, we don't always understand His will. The only way to get through such a swamp is to identify the stones, the patches of dry ground, and step from one to another until we reach the other side. The danger is saying, "I'm stuck. I don't understand. I can't move until I get this figured out." That is a sure way to remain mired in the swamp.

During my battle with cancer twenty years ago, I never knew what the next day would bring. So I focused on what I did know, what I could always anticipate and depend on: God is good; God is love;

God's Word is true; God causes all things to work together for my good according to His purpose; God is conforming me to the image of Christ; God has given me wonderful family and friends—I could find more than enough patches of "dry ground" to step on as I made my way through the swamp of the imponderables every day. Eventually I reached the other side. (And I still don't understand everything that happened in the swamp!)

Don't focus on what you don't understand; focus on what you do. When you feel weak, trust in God's unfailing power to bring you through. In 2 Corinthians 12:9 we are promised: "My grace is all you need. My power works best in weakness" (NLT). That is a good reminder when you are in the swamp of the imponderables.

> *Trusting God means letting stress points become rest points in the road of life.*

Is it possible that God has forgotten about me?

Forgetting is a human experience; it is only natural to wonder if God forgets as well. It is part of the human tendency to create God in our image by wondering if He shares in our frailties. Even the best of human fathers can forget important details of life, so why shouldn't a heavenly Father overlook our needs at times? The Bible sets us straight quickly when it ascribes to God what we humans do to keep from forgetting important things. We write them down—and so does He! Not literally, of course; that is the way the biblical writers suggest that God never forgets: "You number my wanderings; put my tears into Your bottle; *are they* not in Your book?" (Psalm 56:8) Not only does God "record" our "wanderings," He knows them, and records them, before we ever take a step (Psalm 139:16). The Bible uses human terms to point out how different God is from us: God never forgets.

We know that in our mind; it's our heart that *feels* forgotten at times. In those situations, it's good to meditate on Psalm 139:1-12 where David says that, even if he wanted to, he couldn't escape God's presence. If

God is everywhere, then He is with you. And if He is with you, He hasn't forgotten you. How could anyone forget someone from whom he is never separated? Even now, because you are His child, He is working in your behalf. For some people, nothing in our world seems stable anymore. Insecurity is written all over our human experience. It is possible to feel bereft and forgotten. But we are not forgotten. Everything is under the control of God the Creator. Feelings of being forgotten are conquered by truths about being remembered. God knows every need you have, even before you ask.

The Bible uses human terms to point out how different God is from us: God never forgets.

What if God puts me in a situation that I don't know how to handle?

The prophet Habakkuk was like we sometimes are: confused. God had called him to be a prophet and speak to the moral and spiritual decline of Jerusalem. Habakkuk was preaching (at God's request), but God wasn't acting and the people weren't repenting. Habakkuk seemed not to be a very successful prophet. So Habakkuk posed questions *to* and received answers *from* God (Habakkuk 1-2), then penned a beautiful confession of faith (Habakkuk 3). Habakkuk's experience is a model for us when God calls us to do something we feel unequipped to handle.

Habakkuk had to decide: Do I trust God? He could only obey and do the best he could—then trust God with everything else. Habakkuk teaches us this important lesson. You worship the One you trust, and you trust the One you know! Habakkuk knew his God, and because of that he could trust Him when he did not understand what He was doing. The way you get through challenging situations is to build a relationship with God so that when things you see around you start to fall apart, the things you can't see hold you together.

God has safely taken His people through the wilderness every time there has been one in their path. It is a reminder that our sufficiency is in God, not in ourselves.

He has shown you, O man, what is good; and what does the LORD require of you but to do justly, to love mercy, and to walk humbly with your God.
~ Micah 6:8

What should I do when God says "No"?

When we pray and the answer is not "Yes," we assume it is "No." And it could be. At the very least, if it is not "Yes," it is "No, not yet." An unsaved child or spouse, a difficult work environment, a dysfunctional extended family, a medical or financial crisis—what are we to do when God says "No"? If you haven't faced such an answer yet, you will. Nothing builds faith like hearing God say, "No—trust Me in this."

You want a solution, but it seems that for now God is saying "No." Everybody goes through it sooner or later—some unresolved problem, some issue that you don't know what to do about. It seems no matter what you try there is no solution on the horizon.

In your time of waiting, let God comfort you. Whether the answer is a definite "No" or a "No, not yet," God's grace is what comforts us and meets our need for strength, provision, endurance, and sacrifice.

While you wait or change direction, let the "God of all comfort" assure your heart and mind that His answer is trustworthy.

The only way to enjoy life in the midst of its uncertainties is to live in the certainty of God.

How can I have patience when I'm in a hurry but God isn't?

Patience is endurance—but not the grit-your-teeth, feet-planted, white-knuckle kind. That may be the world's way of being patient, but God has a different way: patience by the power of the Holy Spirit. Galatians 5:22-23 says, "But the fruit of the Spirit is love, joy, peace, patience . . . " (NASB). Those attributes are the character of Christ being lived out through the Christian—Christ living in us (Galatians 2:20). So it is not us bending our human will to adjust to God's timetable. It is us allowing God to live out His timetable through us by the presence of the Spirit in us. Patience never means sitting still in frustration. Patience is moving as the Spirit leads and discovering what God is doing every step of the way.

The apostle Paul was a man on a mission, "impatient" from a personality perspective. When he wanted to preach in Asia, the Spirit said "No." When he wanted to preach in Mysia, the Spirit said "No" (Acts 16:6-8). There is no indication of frustration on

Paul's part at these obstacles. He just kept moving until the Spirit said "Yes"—which is how the Gospel made its way into Europe (verses 9-10). Instead of arguing with God, Paul stayed in step with God and was soon shown a new plan. God was in just as big a "hurry" as Paul was (to use human terms). It just took active patience on Paul's part to wait until God made His plans clear.

I have discovered that patience is connected to trust in a cumulative way. Every time I am called on to be patient, and I yield to the Spirit in that moment, it becomes easier the next time. Since God is faithful, there is always a good reason, usually seen in hindsight, for why I needed to wait. Those reasons from the past become reasons in the present. Every time we trust God we accumulate new reasons to trust Him again.

> *If you are waiting to hear from God right now, be patient. The word "late" is not found in the language of heaven.*

Is there hope for this world?

Of course there is hope! The apostle Paul wrote that otherwise, "Our preaching *is* empty and your faith *is* also empty. . . . If in this life only we have hope in Christ, we are of all men the most pitiable" (1 Corinthians 15:14, 19). Paul was talking about eternal hope based on the Resurrection, but working backward it applies to temporal hope as well. In short, our hope lies in the preaching of the truth of the Word of God. The more people respond, the more nations will be changed and become seats of righteousness. This world operates today on the basis that there are no transcendent values which are absolute. Many nations and cultures have adopted a new morality, an amorality which says nothing is right or wrong. Without the transcendent values that come from God, there is no hope. Christ, living through Christians, is the only hope for this world.

Ultimately, our hope is not in a reformed world but in the plans of God for a redeemed world—a new heaven and a new earth (Revelation 21:1). The Bible clearly says that this present world is passing away (1 John 2:17) and will be renovated by fire (2 Peter 3:7). But what of the interim? Are we to give up hope for righteousness, holiness, and justice to prevail? Not at all! We live under an explicit commission and command from Jesus Christ. The commission is to spread the Gospel and make disciples in all nations (Matthew 28:18-20), and the command is to love one another as Christ has loved us (John 13:34). We are to be salt and light in this world, preserving it and illuminating the world's only hope, Jesus Christ (Matthew 5:13-16).

Our hope for this world lies outside of this world— our hope is in the Lord.

> *Moral and spiritual decline happens to individuals before it happens to nations.*

> **Why does it seem like good things always happen to bad people?**

Asaph, the writer of Psalm 73, thought this was happening around him. He saw wicked people who *appeared* to be prosperous. But what he really saw was the appearance of prosperity; he incorrectly judged that the wicked were thriving while he was not. Asaph was looking at the assets of his friends and making subtle evaluations about the importance of life. But when he stopped looking at their possessions and viewed these individuals from God's perspective, something happened. He began to see the lives of these people in their totality. He saw that they would ultimately perish and all their possessions with them: "When I thought *how* to understand [these things], it *was* too painful for me—until I went into the sanctuary of God; *then* I understood their end" (verses 16-17).

Asaph's perspective shifted—it moved out of the realm of the natural and into the realm of the spiritual. Suddenly he saw the future judgment of these people he thought were so successful. He discovered that without God, man cannot have inner strength and that what looks like success is often just a mirage. He wrote, "But *it is* good for me to draw near to God; I have put my trust in the Lord GOD" (Psalm 73:28). We need to take the words of Jesus to heart: "For what profit is it to a man if he gains the whole world, and loses his own soul? Or what will a man give in exchange for his soul?" (Matthew 16:26) Our focus needs to remain on what is eternally unshakeable, not what is here today but will be gone tomorrow.

> *The only passport we need to eternity is Jesus.*

If I have God, then why am I not successful like my friends?

Successful in what way? When Christians ask that question, they are usually focused on one means of measuring success: wealth and material prosperity. And there is no more faulty guide for measuring success than money, biblically speaking. God has gifted some people with business or financial ability, and there is nothing at all wrong with that. But the true measure of success in life is not how much money *you* have but how much of *you* your money has. Regardless of how much material wealth you have, money can have a grip on your soul.

All good gifts come from God (1 Chronicles 29:14; James 1:17), and we should thank Him for the enjoyment they provide. But we have to remember: The Christian's agenda in life is not the same as the world's. We are not in a contest to accumulate as much as we can while we live. We serve a Savior who lived a sacrificial life in order to bring salvation to the world. And that is how His followers measure success as well. But spreading the Gospel takes money, and God has blessed many people who give generously to the Lord instead of accumulating more and more wealth for themselves. We will have all eternity to enjoy riches and blessings far beyond what this world has to offer. For now, remember that the world likes to talk about how much things cost, while God talks about what things are worth— measured against the backdrop of eternity.

The riches of grace are not affected by the stock market or economic conditions—they represent wealth we cannot lose.

Why do bad things happen to good people?

First, the Bible says "there is none who does good, no, not one" (Romans 3:12). That means we have all been tainted by sin and are deserving of the ultimate "bad thing," God's judgment. Actually, the question is not, "Why do bad things happen to good people?" but, "Why does anything good happen to anybody?" Nothing does except by the grace and mercy of God.

Rephrasing the question, we do wonder, "Why do people who are trying to serve the Lord and do the right things experience tragedies? Why doesn't God protect them?" Job is the ultimate example of an eminently righteous person losing everything. But he refused to curse God. Instead, he asked the right question: "Shall we indeed accept good from God, and shall we not accept adversity?" (Job 2:10) Job knew there was an answer to the "why?" question buried somewhere in the counsel of God. And that is what we must depend on as well.

The answer to our "why" questions lies in the One we trust; we trust in God's ultimate lordship over heaven and earth. God is loving and His gifts abound in our world. Our insights are faulty, our perspective limited, our minds small. There is a broader reality that God, in His omniscience, understands perfectly. That's why Proverbs 3:5 tells us to "trust in the LORD with all your heart, and lean not on your own understanding." The word "why" occurs 22 times in the book of Job. Even though Job had far more questions than answers, he kept affirming and reaffirming his faith. He said, "Though He slay me, yet will I trust Him" (Job 13:15). If our faith doesn't work in the darkness, it won't be worth much in the light.

> *Cling to the knowledge that you could be in no safer place than in a storm of His making.*

How can we fight and overcome corruption in our world?

The answer to the corruption and sin in our world is found in the transformation of the human heart. Jesus said, "For from within, out of the heart of men, proceed evil thoughts, adulteries, fornications, murders, thefts, covetousness, wickedness, deceit, lewdness, an evil eye, blasphemy, pride, foolishness. All these evil things come from within and defile a man" (Mark 7:21-23). The Church of Jesus Christ has the only message guaranteed to reveal a man's heart to himself and provide the power for it to be changed (Hebrews 4:12).

Corruption in cultures is nothing but a mirror reflecting the hearts of its citizens. If there is ungodliness in societies it is only because people want it or allow it. Only when people are born-again from above by God's Spirit do they gain a kingdom perspective of this world. Until that happens, all morals are relative and are subject to the whims of the people. Cultures cannot be changed by force. As Paul wrote, the Church's weapons are not worldly or carnal; they are the truths of God's Word that have the power to demolish the lies of Satan (2 Corinthians 10:3-5). Our best strategy for reversing the decline in our culture is to live pure lives ourselves, pray (2 Chronicles 7:14), and continue to proclaim the heart-changing Gospel of Christ.

The simplest witness can dramatically change the world in ways that can only be realized in eternity.

Why are wars continuously erupting in our world?

Conflicts between individuals are called disagreements; conflicts between nations are called wars. The latter is but the former on a grander scale. That doesn't mean that all wars are avoidable. Sometimes evil can only be restrained by the use of defensive and offensive force. Christ Himself will engage in a massive final war at His Second Coming to defeat the armies of the Antichrist (Revelation 19:11). Wars erupt in our world for the same reason that disagreements erupt between individuals: greed, carnal agendas, desire, evil, anger, selfishness, and more. At present, "the whole world lies *under the sway of* the wicked one" (1 John 5:19). It is not insignificant that Satan's last act on earth will be to organize a military rebellion against the Millennium rule of Christ (Revelation 20:7-9). Given the chance, Satan will continue to pit nation against nation in attempts to disrupt the proclamation of the Gospel and the possibility of righteousness being established among nations. Until Christ returns there will be "wars and rumors of wars" on earth (Matthew 24:6).

PERSONAL
BATTLES

But may the God of all grace, who called us to His eternal glory by Christ Jesus, after you have suffered a while, perfect, establish, strengthen, and settle *you*.

1 Peter 5:10

GUILT

> **Is guilt real, or am I just overthinking things?**

The Bible teaches us that guilt is a reality. But two realities need to be separated: Guilt and *feelings* of guilt. If we are actually guilty, we will also feel guilty. But not all feelings of guilt are because we are truly guilty. We can be made to feel guilty by others, we can feel guilt over something that wasn't our fault, and so forth. The Bible addresses true guilt—offending the righteous standards of God by thought, word, or deed.

The Bible says "all have sinned and fall short of the glory of God" (Romans 3:23), so every human being is legitimately guilty. But Christ's death on the cross removed the guilt of man's sin before God for all those who will accept the gift of God's forgiveness (Colossians 2:14). Christ became guilty in our place and suffered the punishment of the cross. Therefore, no matter what sin any Christian has committed, no matter what condemnation you may have felt, or what guilt and shame you may have experienced, the guilt of that sin has been removed. The only way to maintain a clear conscience and avoid the shame of guilt is to continually confess sin to God and receive His forgiveness (1 John 1:9). There is no sin so great that God will not forgive. When you come to God acknowledging your sin and guilt, God will remove your sin, and your joy will be restored.

Confession means admitting our guilt; repentence means we turn around and go the other way.

What steps should I take to eliminate guilt in my life?

If you want to know how to deal with guilt in your life, there is a way out of your desperation. For almost a year, King David lived with the guilt of adultery, deceit, and being an accomplice to murder. To begin his process of restoration, the first thing he did was accept full responsibility for his sin and acknowledge the sinfulness of his actions. That's where restoration begins. Then he made his confession to Almighty God. In Psalm 32:5 David said, "I acknowledged my sin to You, and my iniquity I have not hidden. I said, 'I will confess my transgressions to the LORD.'" Psalm 51 is a longer account of David restoring his relationship with God: his brokenness (verse 17), confession (verses 3-4), cleansing (verses 7-9), and consecration (verses 11-16). Any Christian who has sinned can follow similar steps to remove the guilt of sin. God will forgive you and the joy of your salvation and your fellowship with Him will be restored.

As David expressed, all guilt is ultimately based on sin against God (Psalm 51:4). But if we have sinned against another person, it is important to seek their forgiveness as well (Matthew 5:23-24). No one can remove guilt except God alone, but confession and forgiveness can restore fellowship among individuals.

Don't be afraid to look closely at your spiritual life so that you may rest confidently in your eternal life.

How can I move on from my guilt?

Once you have made your confession to God and your fellowship is renewed, you need to begin focusing on the future. King David is a worthy example of the fact that sin and forgiveness are in the past tense. Once he had confessed his sin to Almighty God, he wrote the following: "Blessed *is he whose* transgression *is* forgiven, *whose* sin is covered. Blessed *is* the man to whom the LORD does not impute iniquity, and in whose spirit *there is* no deceit" (Psalm 32:1-2). After David's ordeal was over, he immediately moved on (2 Samuel 12:20). That may seem abrupt, but it illustrates a point: God's forgiveness is a response to repentance and confession. Once granted, we should move forward with life. Yes, there may be time needed for restoration and reconciliation, but that should happen immediately. Only Satan would want to keep a forgiven person bogged down with feelings of guilt and shame.

David wrote, "Blessed *is he whose* transgression *is* forgiven." The Hebrew word for "blessed" means "happy." Indeed, happy is the person who can move forward knowing that sin and resulting guilt can be left in the past. There is nothing like the knowledge that you have been forgiven.

Agreeing with God is always good for the soul.

DEPRESSION AND ANXIETY

Is it a sin for Christians to be depressed?

There are some who believe a Christian should never suffer from depression. But that is incorrect. The lines between sad, discouraged, depressed, and similar conditions are too fuzzy to say a Christian can be discouraged but not depressed, or sad but not depressed. The reality is, depression afflicts many people, Christians included. Many biblical characters exhibited signs that would likely be classified as depression using modern definition— Abraham, Jonah, Job, Jeremiah, Elijah and others. King David, a man after God's own heart, wrote, "I am troubled, I am bowed down greatly; I go mourning all the day long. . . . I groan because of the turmoil of my heart"(Psalm 38:6-8). In Psalm 42 and

43, the psalmist asks, "Why are you cast down, O my soul? And why are you disquieted within me?"

There are moments in life when our souls are sad. It is not a sin to experience depression as a Christian, though it is possible that depression could be linked to underlying, unconfessed sin. When we are disquieted in our soul, we are counseled to "hope in God" (Psalm 43:5). With God's help, Christians can successfully weather the storms of life—even depression. "*The righteous* cry out, and the LORD hears, and delivers them out of all their troubles" (Psalm 34:17).

The more you reach out to other people with needs, the smaller your fears become.

Why do people get depressed?

Depression can be directly linked to something that has happened in our lives—a personal loss, a mistake, guilt, unconfessed sin, ongoing stress, or some other event. That kind of depression can be addressed by dealing with the root event, bringing freedom and release from symptoms.

For some people, depression can also have physiological roots—something to do with what's going on in their physical body, such as a chemical or hormonal imbalance, a genetic or postpartum condition, dietary issues, or lack of sleep. These disorders can certainly impact one's mood and require assistance from a medical professional. Such causes should be screened for by a doctor and treated medically if discovered.

Sometimes there are satanic reasons for depression. Satan cannot possess a Christian, but he can certainly torment by planting seeds of doubt concerning God's love, care, forgiveness, approval, and acceptance. Satan's chief goal is to get the believer to lose confidence in God as he tried to do with Job (Job 1:11; 2:5). He will come and say, "God doesn't love you as much as He used to," or "God doesn't care about you," or "He's not really interested in your pain." Just as a child who is rejected by her parents may suffer long-term effects, a Christian who believes God has rejected her could show symptoms of depression. When restoring and maintaining sound mental and emotional health, distinguishing between the lies of Satan and the truth of God is imperative.

Regardless of the event or attack, depression is not a foregone conclusion for the follower of Christ. As Paul expressed, "*We are* hard-pressed on every side, yet not crushed; *we are* perplexed, but not in despair; persecuted, but not forsaken; struck down, but not destroyed. . . . Therefore we do not lose heart. Even though our outward *man* is perishing, yet the inward man is being renewed day by day" (2 Corinthians 4:8-9, 16).

How can I eliminate depression in my life?

With God's help, you can make inroads to eliminating depression from your life. Here are some steps to take when battling depression:

• Engage: You must see depression as an enemy and *engage* it; you must battle it. Whatever the cause or source of depression, it is not from God; He does not want you to be cast down. You must engage depression actively, not wait for it to disappear passively. Ask the Holy Spirit to guide you and gird you with His power and wisdom in this battle.

• Eliminate: *Eliminate* any identifiable possible source of the depression, including medical reasons by a checkup with your doctor. Is there unconfessed sin? Have you been hurt by another person? Is there bitterness, anger, envy, or discontentment? By eliminating causes—with the help of a trusted counselor, if needed—you may discover the cause.

• Exercise: Regular physical exercise (check with your doctor if necessary) releases hormones into the body that have a positive effect—like the "runner's high." The cardiovascular benefit of increased blood flow means more oxygen to the brain providing clarity and energy. In addition to exercising physically, make sure you are exercising spiritually: regular prayer, Bible study, worship, and interaction with others is part of a *healthy* Christian life.

• Expect: *Expect* that God wants you to be joyful and free from depression. Meditate on the fruit of the Spirit (Galatians 5:22-23) and ask the Spirit to manifest the life of Christ through you. Believe that "all things *are* possible to him who believes" (Mark 9:23). Believe that it is God's will for you to be free of depression and that by asking, you will receive that freedom (John 14:13).

• Edify: Use your spiritual gift(s), given by God, to serve the body of Christ. Put your focus on edifying others. This is not an avoidance or denial tactic; it is another dimension to being blessed by doing God's will through service. You are less likely to feel depressed when you are helping others than if you are isolated and inwardly focused.

• Enjoy: If sadness or depression has taken you out of social contact with family, friends, or peers, get back in the loop! *Enjoy* the life God has given you. If it is true that your heart follows your treasure (Matthew 6:19-21), see if your heart won't also follow your body as you re-engage with your social networks—especially those who have your spiritual and emotional well-being in mind.

• Elevate: Depend on God to help you "mount up with wings like eagles" as He renews your strength day by day (Isaiah 40:31).

Accepting God's opinion of you in Christ is the first step toward self-acceptance.

God knows my pain, so why bother praying for help?

This objection to prayer applies to any subject, not just depression. If God already knows our needs before we pray—and He does (Matthew 6:8)— why should we pray at all? The general answer, regardless of the subject, is because we are told to pray. Jesus taught His disciples to pray, which is a good reason for us to follow suit (Matthew 6:9-13).

Specifically, regarding prayer to relieve emotional pain or depression, we should pray because of the promise of Philippians 4:6-7. If there is one thing a depressed person needs perhaps more than anything, it is peace—peace of mind and heart. And that is what Scripture promises when we commit our needs to God: "Be anxious for nothing, but in everything by prayer and supplication, with thanksgiving, let your requests be made known to God; and the peace of God, which surpasses all understanding, will guard your hearts and minds through Christ Jesus." God is there and He cares about us. We can tell Him anything. When feeling anxious, commit your anxiety to God in prayer with thanksgiving. Then let the peace of God guard your heart and mind. Exchange anxiety for peace through prayer.

True prayer in the time of trouble resigns to God's will.

Is there any way to prevent anxiety?

Anxiety and depression are struggles that take place on the battlefield of the mind. To avoid anxiety, we must think proper thoughts. Most people don't realize that thinking should be a discipline like prayer or Bible study. We are in control of our thoughts and can choose what we contemplate. Yes, thoughts can pop into our mind—but we are not obligated to dwell on them. But certain kinds of thoughts are worthy of our contemplation, and the apostle Paul gives us six examples (Philippians 4:8-9):

• Things that are *true*: Think about *real* things. Don't indulge in fantasy, dread, worry, or things over which you have no control. Make sure you're dealing with reality.

• Things that are *noble*: Dwell on honorable and uplifting things, not dishonorable (impure, violent, hurtful, shameful, sinful).

• Things that are *just*: Entertain thoughts about

things that are righteous by both divine and human standards.

• Things that are *pure*: We should guard our minds against impure thoughts, subjects, and images.

• Things that are *lovely*: This is the only time that the word "lovely" appears in the New Testament, a Greek word that means "pleasing and orderly." Beauty and order reflect creation and the Creator.

• Things that are of *good report*: In short, reputable things. We shouldn't think about things we would be unwilling to speak about to those we respect.

Paul summarizes by saying we should fill our minds with thoughts of "virtuous" and "praiseworthy" subjects. If we follow these exhortations, "the God of peace will be with [us]" (verse 9). Do you see how the mind is a battlefield? Consider how many thoughts come to your mind daily—from media and from your own heart—that are *not* consistent with Paul's ideals. Maintaining a positive, peaceful, uplifting frame of mind is a daily challenge. But through prayer and proper thinking, the peace of God can be ours.

DISHONESTY

Should I tell the truth even when it hurts someone?

The notion of "situational ethics" was popularized in American culture in the 1960s and 1970s. The idea was that "the way of love" was the supreme ethic—that it would be better to tell a lie if it would spare someone unnecessary pain or grief. To cause someone pain by telling the truth would not be loving. Therefore, the situation determines the ethics; there is no moral absolute when it comes to telling the truth or not. That simplistic thinking overlooks the fact that there are always other alternatives to being untruthful—and there are often a multitude of consequences when we aren't truthful.

The Bible combines truth and love into a different ethic when it encourages "speaking the truth in love" (Ephesians 4:15). Therefore, we are not left with an either/or choice—either truth or love—but we are given a both/and solution: Speak the truth in a loving way. Truth is fundamental to the character of God and godly persons. The prohibition to giving false testimony (bearing false witness) was the ninth of God's Ten Commandments to Israel (Exodus 20:16), and Jesus called Himself "the truth" in John 14:6. On the other hand, Jesus noted that it is the nature of Satan to lie: "There is no truth in him. . . . for he is a liar and the father of it" (John 8:44).

Because of our fallen nature, we are born into this world as confirmed liars. Telling the truth is something we learn—sometimes the hard way! Once you tell a lie, your character is tarnished in a way that can take years to recover. Once others realize you have been willing to deceive, how can they have confidence in anything you say?

When Paul says to speak the truth "in love," he uses the Greek word (*agape*) for selfless love, love that thinks more of the welfare of others than of self. So, if it is necessary to speak a hard truth, we do it with compassion and humility. In the long-term, telling a lie (or withholding the truth) is in no one's best interest. But a word of caution: Speaking the truth should never be a license to gossip. Truth should be spoken only to those who need to hear it.

Speak the truth in love.

How can I become a person who always speaks the truth?

Even after we become Christians, telling the truth is continually a discipline that we must practice and put into place. Though we are new creatures in Christ (2 Corinthians 5:17), we are daily putting off old ways and putting on new ways (Ephesians 4:24). One of those new ways of living is being a person of truth—a person who is transparent and honest, who practices no deceit of any kind. The conscience plays a role. To the degree a person's conscience was conditioned to accept lies as tolerable, to that degree the challenge to recondition the conscience in accord with God's standards may be harder. The more intimate you become with God and His Word, the more sensitive you become to straying from the truth in any way: lies, exaggerations, presumptions, deceit, partial truths, and the like.

First, feed your mind on God's Word, "the entirety of [which] is truth" (Psalm 119:160). Second, "[choose] the way of truth" (Psalm 119:30). If you stray from the truth, correct it immediately. Be diligent about living a true life. Third, be filled with "the Spirit of truth" (John 14:17). Do not grieve the Spirit by the way you speak or live (Ephesians 4:29-30). Fourth, confess any lies you have told to others and seek forgiveness (Colossians 3:9). Fifth, pursue spiritual maturity in every dimension, especially through prayer, so your "senses [are] exercised to discern both good and evil" (Hebrews 5:14). It's not complicated. Just draw a line in the sand, right here on this day, and whatever your habits have been, from now on, resolve to tell the truth.

The truth will make you free.

IMMORALITY

> **Is it okay to sin since God will forgive me anyway?**

As a follower of Christ, we should never willingly wish to grieve the heart of God by sinning. In his letter to the Romans, Paul clearly states that we are not free to disregard God's moral laws just because we live under grace. He wrote, "How shall we who died to sin live any longer in it?" (Romans 6:1-2) Grace does not mean that we are free to do what we want but that we are empowered to do what we ought. We are fully obligated to keep God's moral and ethical laws not because we are saved by doing so, but because they represent His character. In the New Testament, we have been given an even higher motivation for fulfilling God's moral law, and that motivation is love. Grace means living a moral life, not because we have to but because we want to—and our motivation is love. "Love is the fulfillment of the law" (Romans 13:10).

Grace isn't the natural way to behave; it's the supernatural way.

Is it wrong to choose my own form of morality?

Throughout the Old Testament, Israel was warned about the folly of worshiping idols carved out of wood or stone by human hands (Daniel 5:23). That is a clear example of man creating God in his own image: We imagine what we think God and His laws should be like, create Him, then worship our creation. The apostle Paul wrote that those who do this—then and now—have "exchanged the truth of God for the lie, and worshiped and served the creature rather than the Creator, who is blessed forever. Amen" (Romans 1:25).

The Christian faith is based on revelation—God revealing Himself to man (Hebrews 1:1-3). Besides what is apparent in nature (Psalm 19:1-6), what we know about God's standards and expectation is revealed in the Bible. It stands as a unified source of morals and ethics from God's point of view. One may change what the Bible says to suit his own moral views, but that is a freedom man *takes*, not one that God *gives*. Where the Bible doesn't provide specific answers to a particular moral question, care must be taken to formulate positions that seem consistent with what the Bible does say. But where the Bible speaks clearly on moral matters, deviating from the biblical path can lead to pain, sorrow, and regret. The question always comes down to the issue of elevating one's personal desires over God's. It is a question of Who or what you love the most—the desire to set oneself as the moral authority or to trust in the moral authority of God as revealed through His Word. Jesus made it clear: One cannot serve God's standards and man's at the same time (Luke 16:13).

Your willingness to be fascinated by the world is your invitation for the world to overwhelm you.

Self-Control

> **Can someone with a reckless tongue also be godly?**

Think about what happened to an ancient city that allowed its walls to crumble and fall down; it was vulnerable to destruction. That's the image King Solomon used to illustrate the danger of a lack of self-control: "*Like* a city whose walls are broken through is a person who lacks self-control" (Proverbs 25:28, NIV 1984). Self-control is the "wall" that protects us from the dangers of temptation, impulsiveness, and hasty speech. Someone has noted that almost every sin is in some way related to the abuse of the tongue. And nothing is harder to control, the Bible says, than the tongue (James 3:1-12). The more we talk, the more likely we are to sin (Proverbs 10:19). That's why James says it is good to be "swift to hear, [and] slow to speak" (James 1:19).

The tongue (speech) can inflict damage far greater than its relative size; it can drastically influence the direction of a life—like a bridle on a horse, a rudder on a ship, or a spark in a forest (James 3:3-6). As far as godliness and a reckless tongue, James says there is a great disconnect between both praises and curses coming out of the same mouth—like salt and fresh water coming out of the same spring, or the same vine or tree bearing both grapes and olives (James 3:9-12). In other words, those who are godly will manifest the character of Christ by the fruit of the Holy Spirit—part of which is self-control (Galatians 5:23). Everything we do should glorify God, and that most definitely includes how we speak.

> *The best way to avoid being defined by this world is to love God with all you are and have.*

Is it wrong to be angry?

A key passage for understanding anger in Scripture is Ephesians 4:26-27: "Be angry, and yet do not sin; do not let the sun go down on your anger, and do not give the devil an opportunity" (NASB). There are apparently options: being angry and sinning, and being angry and *not* sinning. The difference is this: Anger without sinning is "righteous indignation," as when Jesus became indignant over how the Jerusalem temple had been turned into a commercial center for the sake of profit (Matthew 21:12-13). On many occasions, the Old Testament prophets were indignant (angry) over social injustice and spiritual apathy in Israel. But sinful anger—that hardly needs an explanation. The difference between the two is this: Sinful anger is *self*-centered, while righteous indignation is *God*-centered. Sinful anger is *hurtful*, while righteous anger is *holy*. Sinful anger seeks *retribution*, while righteous anger seeks *repentance*. Sinful anger gives the *devil* an opportunity, while righteous anger gives *God* an opportunity.

Unfortunately, there is more sinful anger in the world than there is righteous indignation. And yes, it is wrong to be sinfully angry. It can be hurtful and destructive to relationships, and harmful to our physical health. We are warned about letting a "root of bitterness" spring up and "cause trouble," defiling many (Hebrews 12:15). The apostle James makes a marked distinction between the two kinds of anger: "For the wrath of man does not produce the righteousness of God" (James 1:20). We cannot justify our sinful anger by claiming to be "righteously indignant." We can be one or the other, but not both at the same time.

When you deal with your anger, you will be more receptive to God and His Word.

TEMPTATION

Does everyone struggle with temptation?

Know that temptation is a common experience for every single person. King Solomon was right when he wrote, "And *there is* nothing new under the sun" (Ecclesiastes 1:9c). Often those who have yielded to temptation will justify their sin by saying, "You don't understand; this was different!" The situation might have been different, but the temptation wasn't. Beginning with Adam and Eve, temptation to sin has plagued the human race. There are no new temptations, only new opportunities to yield or resist. The apostle Paul spoke to the commonness of temptation this way: "No temptation has overtaken you except such as is common to man"

(1 Corinthians 10:13a). Temptation is the common enemy of every person living on earth. The ultimate proof that everyone struggles with temptation is the fact that Jesus was tempted by the devil at the beginning of His ministry (Matthew 4:1-11) and "was in all *points* tempted as *we are, yet* without sin" (Hebrews 4:15b). Jesus' victory over sin, the world, and the devil would not have been authentic if He were not genuinely tempted to sin. Just as the first Adam was tempted and sinned, the last Adam was tempted but did not sin.

Fortunately, though *all* are tempted to sin, none *have* to sin: "But God *is* faithful, who will not allow you to be tempted beyond what you are able, but with the temptation will also make the way of escape, that you may be able to bear *it*" (1 Corinthians 10:13b). When some say, "I gave in; I couldn't bear the temptation," they contradict the Word of God. His promise is to *always* provide a way of escape.

Is temptation a sin?

The simple answer is, No—temptation is not a sin. *Yielding to temptation* is sin; *temptation* is not sin. If temptation were a sin, then Jesus Himself could not have died as a sinless Savior because He was tempted: "for we do not have a High Priest who cannot sympathize with our weaknesses, but was in all *points* tempted as *we are, yet* without sin" (Hebrews 4:15). The temptation the Lord experienced was not a sin. Though He was tempted, He was without sin. We can't stop thoughts (temptations) from coming into our mind, but that doesn't mean we have to yield to them. Martin Luther, the father of the Protestant Reformation, is credited with noting, "You can't stop birds from flying overhead, but you can stop them from building a nest in your hair."

> *Jesus Christ was tempted in every area just as we are tempted, yet He never sinned.*

Is there really a purpose for temptation?

You might think you would be better off without temptation, but that's not true. There is a purpose for temptation. Think of Adam and Eve in the Garden of Eden. What was the purpose of their temptation? Ultimately, it was a test of their allegiance to God; it was a test of their faith and obedience. And the price was high—the destiny of the entire human race hung in the balance. Because they yielded to temptation and sinned, it became necessary for God to provide the opportunity for redemption. He sent His Son, Jesus Christ, as the "last Adam" to succeed where the first Adam failed (1 Corinthians 15:45). Jesus' threefold victory over Satan in the wilderness was a repeat of the first Adam's test in Eden. Jesus was victorious in that test of His obedience and remained victorious for the next three years, securing the right to be the unblemished "Lamb of God who takes away the sin of the world!" (John 1:29)

As for us, the purpose of temptation is the same. Whenever you face temptation, and you are victorious over it, it builds the strength of your spiritual muscles so you have the strength for the next time it comes. James wrote, "My brethren, count it all joy when you fall into various trials [temptations], knowing that the testing of your faith produces patience" (James 1:2-3). The Greek word for "trials" can also be translated "temptations." James says that trials are tests of our faith. They become temptations when we are tempted to respond to a trial in an ungodly way. Temptations give us the opportunity to see the condition of our own heart. Temptation reveals what's in our heart. It is the route God uses to approve our life. God gives us a choice just as Adam, Eve, and Jesus had a choice. While the fate of the world does not hinge on our response to temptation, our response is still important. It will dramatically impact the destiny of our life, that of our family, or others. We need to view temptation seriously as an opportunity to prove to ourselves and to God the depth of our commitment to Him.

Will I ever be tempted beyond what I can handle?

No. We must remember that temptations are filtered through the permission of God. God put a hedge of protection around Job, allowing him to be touched only up to a point (Job 1-2). In the same way, "God . . . *will not allow* you to be tempted beyond what you are able, but with the temptation will also make the way of escape, that you may be able to bear *it*" (1 Corinthians 10:13, italics added). God knows you and knows what you are "able" to handle. That means every temptation is an opportunity for victory! If we can't be tempted beyond our ability, then we will be able to resist. Temptation is not based on what *we think* we can handle; it is based on what *God knows* we can handle.

God will provide a way of escape if we will take it. The word for "escape" that Paul uses in 1 Corinthians 10:13 suggests a narrow passageway, like a path leading between the steep walls of a canyon. There's only one way out; if we are to escape the temptation, it will be by the way of escape God provides. It is up to us to see it and to take it.

Building reserves of strength through resisting temptation will align our will with God's.

Will I experience temptation throughout my entire life?

As long as we live in this world with all of its influences and struggles, we are always going to be exposed to temptation. This verse from the apostle Paul should dispel any notion that a Christian can ever relax regarding temptation: "Therefore let him who thinks he stands take heed lest he fall" (1 Corinthians 10:12). Why did Paul issue that warning? Because he had just recounted some times in Israel's history when the nation fell into serious sin because they let down their guard. And Paul says, "Now these things became our examples, to the intent that we should not lust after evil things as they also lusted" (verse 6). (And speaking of personal lust and desire—that is the origin of sin according to James 1:13-15. If you have desires, you qualify to be tempted.) Age, maturity, years of being a Christian, position, past spiritual success—all these could be reasons that we, like Israel, could let down our guard and yield to desires. Four times in the New Testament, Christians are warned, "Do not be deceived" (James 1:16). Anyone who thinks he is immune to falling into sin is already ripe for a fall (Proverbs 16:18).

The Bible gives us no reason to think there is anything we can ever do to make all temptation go away. And I happen to believe that as we become more mature in the Lord, as we grow in the Lord, the temptations become more subtle and sometimes more intense. The more impact one is having for Christ, the more Satan would like to negate that person's impact with temptations.

The Bible's best and brightest weren't heroes for their doubts; they were heroes for confronting and conquering them.

DEFEATING THE ENEMY

How can I defeat the enemy?

Let's begin with this thought: Did Satan ever gain victory over Christ? No. Therefore, if we are in Christ, can Satan gain victory over us? No. The only variable* is to remain steadfast in our obedience to Christ and His Spirit, never giving the devil an "opportunity" (Ephesians 4:27, NASB). There are two dimensions to being "in Christ." One is positional—we are in Christ by virtue of dying and being resurrected with Him to new life (Romans 6:1-14). That part is what God has done. That position frees us from slavery to sin and temptation. Practically, we are to "put on the Lord Jesus Christ, and make no provision for the flesh, to *fulfill its* lusts" (Romans 13:14). That part is what *we* must do. We do that best by "putting on" the spiritual armor God has provided every Christian: truth, righteousness, peace, faith, salvation, and the Word of God (Ephesians 6:10-18). Clothed in that armor—clothed with Christ—we can defeat the snares and strategies of the devil.

Peter and James add practical insights into defeating Satan. Peter writes that we must be "sober" and "vigilant" because "the devil walks about like a roaring lion, seeking whom he may devour." There is an attitude we must adopt. We must be watchful. We are to be alert about the schemes and plans of Satan so that we do not become caught up in his strategies and snares. Peter's version of being clothed in spiritual armor is more succinct: "Resist [the devil], steadfast in the faith . . ." (1 Peter 5:8-9). James says nearly the same: "Therefore submit to God. Resist the devil and he will flee from you. Draw near to God and He will draw near to you" (James 4:7-8a). The effect of the apostles' teaching is that the devil is defeatable and resistible for those who live and abide in Christ (John 15:7).

How does Satan disguise himself?

The apostle Paul divides the world into two categories: darkness and light. Christians have been rescued from the dominion of darkness (Satan's realm) and brought into the kingdom of light (God's kingdom) (Colossians 1:12-14). If Satan wants access to Christians—"children of light" (Ephesians 5:8)—he and his workers will have to disguise themselves; they will have to conceal their darkness with a covering of light. And that is exactly how Paul describes them: "For such are false apostles, deceitful workers, transforming themselves into apostles of Christ. And no wonder! For Satan himself transforms himself into an angel of light. Therefore it is no great thing if his ministers also transform themselves into ministers of righteousness, whose end will be according to their works" (2 Corinthians 11:13-15).

In the same clever way that Satan's emissaries disguised themselves sufficiently to infiltrate the church at Corinth, so do they disguise themselves today—but not just in the Church. Their work is evident in society at large. Just as the Gospel of Christ and the grace of God bring light into the darkness (John 1:1-9), so Satan disguises himself to hide his dark motives in all realms of society: education, medicine, academics, psychology, music, art, entertainment, and more. That is, everywhere God has and is bringing light into the world, Satan is disguising his lies as a version of truth in order to gain access and a hearing. That is why when you turn on the television, the satanic things that come to corrupt the lives of people are never shown in darkness and despair. There are no warning signs posted that state, "Beware, this could be destructive to your spiritual health." Satan's lures are staged in attractive settings with all of the enticement possible in light of who Satan is.

Every Christian is to be discerning about what they embrace in this world—to make sure it is true light and not darkness in disguise.

> *Nothing gets into our heart accidentally.*

Mistakes and Forgiveness

> **How can I come to genuinely confess my sins?**

A bit of etymology—word origins—can help us answer this question. The Greek word for "confession" is *homologeo,* and it means "to speak the same" or "to agree, admit, or confess." So at the heart of confession is agreeing with God, or saying the same thing about our sins as God says, to acknowledge you're wrong. You may say, "That's so hard." But it is the only way back. When we come to God to ask for forgiveness, our confession needs to be genuine. When we do that, the Bible says God "is faithful and just to forgive us our sins and to cleanse us from all unrighteousness" (1 John 1:9).

The danger comes when we redefine our actions to make them seem less offensive. Instead of calling a lack of self-control "impulsiveness," or calling anger "emotionalism," or calling a lie an "exaggeration," we should agree with God and call them what He calls them. He already knows what we did, so it does little good to describe our sins in a less offensive way.

Confession is a humbling act. When King David confessed his sins to God, he knew what God wanted was a "broken spirit, a broken and contrite heart" (Psalm 51:17). So that's what he brought to his confession. He said that God "will not despise" such an attitude (verse 17), which suggests that confessing our sins without a broken and contrite heart is not what God wants.

The apostle Paul drew a distinction between confessing *with* godly sorrow and *without*. The sorrow of the world means "I'm sorry I got caught," while godly sorrow produces repentance that says, "I'm truly sorry for my thoughts, words, and deeds" (2 Corinthians 7:9-10). Godly sorrow that leads to confession and repentance is an outgrowth of living with humble appreciation for the grace and holiness of God.

Once I'm forgiven for my sins, shouldn't my life return to normal?

Two realms are involved in sin, confession, and forgiveness: heavenly and earthly. From heaven's perspective, the Bible is clear that, when we confess, God forgives our sins and cleanses us from unrighteousness (1 John 1:9). That isn't a drawn-out process; we truly repent and confess and God forgives.

On earth, things are different. Though sins happen in a moment of time, they are preceded by a pattern of carelessness, disobedience, or letting down one's guard; sins are the result of choices *over* time as well as choices *in* time. And time is involved after confession and forgiveness as well. Just as a pattern of living allowed a sin to happen, it will take time to replace that pattern of living with a pattern of godliness. And where other people are involved, it will take time for relationships to be restored and restitution to be made. People can, like God, offer genuine forgiveness in a moment of time. But life doesn't always "return to normal" immediately. Old habits must be unlearned, and new habits of godliness must replace them—and that process takes time. God's goal is not just to *forgive* our past but to *forge* a new future for His children. And that takes time and commitment.

> *God's goal is not just to* **forgive** *our past but to* **forge** *a new future for His children.*

Does God give second chances?

How about 490 chances? When Peter asked Jesus whether he should be so extravagant as to forgive another person as many as seven times, Jesus answered, "Up to seventy times seven" times (Matthew 18:21-22)—that's 490 times! "Seventy times seven" wasn't literal, of course. It was Jesus' way of saying, "Stop counting; just forgive." If the Son of God suggested there should be no limit on human forgiveness—human "second chances"— it seems likely that He was reflecting heaven's standards about forgiveness.

Our God is a God of second chances. Scripture is filled with examples of God giving people the opportunity to start fresh in life. Jonah was a disobedient prophet; Moses was a murderer; David was an adulterer, deceiver, and co-conspirator in murder; the Prodigal Son was greedy and disrespectful; Mark was a quitter; Peter was fearful and a liar; Timothy was timid; and the list goes on. If you have ever sinned and been forgiven, then you can add your name to that list. God gives unlimited opportunities for us to continue growing "in the grace and knowledge of our Lord and Savior Jesus Christ" (2 Peter 3:18).

But there is often a time of instruction after a time of failure. The writer to the Hebrews devotes a lengthy section of his letter to the topic of God's discipline and the purposes for it—"that *we* may be partakers of His holiness" (Hebrews 12:1-13; verse 10). God will use different ways of strengthening us, correcting us, and preparing us to reenter His service. Failure is not final—but it is serious. And it has consequences. God takes every measure to help us not repeat the past. The Christian life is a process of progress. God will repeat the process as often as needed until we are conformed to the image of His Son (Romans 8:29).

> *Our God is a God of second chances.*

Will God ever stop loving me?

There are two parts to this question: Will God ever stop loving—and, Will God ever stop loving *me?* The answer to both is "No," as Scripture clearly states.

First, "God is love" (1 John 4:16). He not only *loves;* He *is* love. When God loves, it is a reflection of who He is, His character and His attributes. If God were ever to stop loving, He would have to deny Himself. But what about His love for individuals? Couldn't God continue to love the world but withdraw His love from me because of my sins? Paul wrote a detailed description of all the things that might possibly separate a Christian from God's love in Christ, only to conclude that none of the them "shall be able to separate us from the love of God which is in Christ Jesus our Lord" (Romans 8:31-39).

I am convinced by experience that one of Satan's greatest strategies is to lie to Christians about the limitations of God's love. Satan will try to make us think God loves us like we love one another— sometimes inconsistently and with limits. Instead of resting in God's unfailing love, Satan would have us squirm in shame over our sins. If we *feel* unloved, we must *focus* on what the Bible says. We must walk by faith, not by feelings (2 Corinthians 5:7). God doesn't love us because of what we do or don't do; God loves us because He is love and it is His nature to love us. He cannot help Himself.

Whatever your circumstances, choose to trust God in the midst of them.

Why should I forgive someone, and not retaliate, if they intentionally hurt me?

There is a deception involved in letting our feelings get the upper hand when we are hurt. We think we are going to feel better after we retaliate against another person, and we might for a moment. But we never ultimately feel better when we do the wrong thing. And vengeance and retaliation are wrong. If ever there was someone who might have felt justified in retaliation against others, it was Joseph. The way he was mistreated by his brothers would, from a purely human perspective, qualify him to seek revenge. But he did not. Joseph could have put himself in God's place and executed judgment upon his brothers, but he said, "Am I in the place of God?" (Genesis 50:19) He knew that vengeance belonged to God alone, not to him (Romans 12:19).

It's easy to forget this when the tables turn. Perhaps you have been at the mercy of your tormentor for the longest of times, and then the roles reverse. Suddenly you find it within your power to exact vengeance on the one who has been your enemy. That's the situation in which Joseph found himself, but he refused to strike. He refused to sit in God's chair and be judge and jury over his brothers (Genesis 45:5-8).

Joseph didn't forgive as a holier-than-thou superior to his brothers. He forgave as one who was compassionate for their situation. He remained kind and tenderhearted throughout his dealings with his brothers. His forgiveness was real because he knew who they were and who he was: flawed human beings who could only be united by genuine forgiveness. Just as Joseph forgave his brothers for their sin and trusted God with the rest, so should we.

Extend forgiveness to others the same way that God did to us: unconditionally.

CHRISTIAN
LIVING

My brethren, count it
all joy when you fall
into various trials,
knowing that the
testing of your faith
produces patience.
But let patience have
its perfect work, that
you may be perfect
and complete,
lacking nothing.

James 1:2-4

COURAGE

> **How can I gain the courage to say no to sin?**

When confronted with a choice to be courageous or to go along with peer or cultural pressures to sin, a good place to begin is the Word of God. It provides a reliable starting point because God's Word is unchanging—you can rely upon its truth to help you remain strong. The phrase "be strong and of good courage" occurs nine times in the Old Testament. God wants us to be strong. When we take a stand for righteousness, it fires the furnace of our own intestinal fortitude to be able to take the next step in faith. God's presence and God's promises are good reasons to have courage when faced with testing. As we are obedient to God and His Word, He will give courage and conviction for future trials. With each victory you experience, you will become stronger in your walk with God.

How can I live an uncompromising life?

Wherever we see compromise, we always see loss, not gain. But the world's message to us in our culture is this: "If you want to get ahead, you are going to have to break a few of the rules to do it." God says you don't have to do that, and Daniel is the perfect example of that. Daniel stands out among biblical characters and heroes for this reason: We have no record of him or his friends ever compromising their faith. Whether it was refusing to violate their Jewish dietary standards (Daniel 1:8-16), refusing to worship the image of the Babylonian king (Daniel 3), or refusing to stop praying to God (Daniel 6), they were resolute in their uncompromising commitment to their beliefs. Daniel was not afraid to speak of God's judgment. He took no thought of the consequences to himself that might come from obeying God. And he was greatly blessed by God.

Daniel illustrates for us how to continue walking uprightly and resolutely with faith in God; whether we are in the political realm, in the church, or whatever our vocation, we need not bend the rules to be blessed by God. But the point is not rewards on earth or rewards in heaven. The point is to follow Daniel's example: "But Daniel purposed in his heart that he would not defile himself" by compromise (Daniel 1:8), to "be strong in the Lord and in the power of His might" (Ephesians 6:10).

> *Success is not dependent upon our compromising what we are committed to. The story of compromise in the Bible is not a happy one. Adam compromised God's law, he followed his wife's sin, and he lost paradise.*

HOPE

How can I fight discouragement?

Many people today are feeling weak and fearful,
and it would be easy to become discouraged; but
the answer to discouragement is to put our trust in
God regardless of our situation. The psalmist—three
times in Psalm 42 and 43—reminded himself to do
just that: "Why are you cast down, O my soul? And
why are you disquieted within me? Hope in God, for I
shall yet praise Him *for* the help of His countenance"
(Psalm 42:5, 11; Psalm 43:5). The psalmist took stock
of his own situation—a cast down, disquieted soul—
and wrote himself a prescription: "I will put my
hope in God; I will praise Him for the help of His
presence." God was there with him, and the psalmist
decided to believe what he knew was true instead

of being discouraged about lesser matters. We have a whole Bible full of truth about God that gives us reason to put our hope in Him. Since we have not been given an exemption from adversity, we must put our faith and trust in Him as we move forward.

The question is not __if__ God will prove Himself faithful to you, but __how__.

I feel like I have no control over my circumstances. Where do I turn?

In our world today, if you don't read the daily newspaper through the lens of God's Word, everything can look pretty dim. It's as if our lives are at the whim of people and forces over which we have no control. Humanly speaking, that's not far from the truth. Leaders we don't know make decisions that radically affect our lives. But this is nothing new. The author of Psalm 146 felt the same way and had good advice: "Do not put your trust in princes, *nor* in a son of man, in whom *there is* no help (verse 3). (It would be foolish to put our hope and trust in fallible political leaders.) Psalm 146 goes on to say, "Happy *is he* who *has* the God of Jacob for his help, whose hope *is* in the LORD his God, who made heaven and earth, the sea, and all that *is* in them; who keeps truth forever, who executes justice for the oppressed . . ." (verses 5-7). When your circumstances look challenging, look to the One who "raises those who are bowed down" (verse 8). His Word never fails—He will lift you up. Resolve to put your hope in God, remembering that man is mortal, but God is immortal; man's truth perishes, but God's truth is forever; man is helpless, but God is our ever present help in times of trouble.

Put your hope in God, remembering that man is mortal, but God is immortal.

Loneliness

How can I escape loneliness?

Loneliness is a state of mind, not a state of place. Being alone is a state of place, where we are. Loneliness is mental and emotional, while being alone is physical. And we have all experienced both; we have been alone and we have felt lonely. Even if we are alone, yet enjoy fruitful and loving relationships in our life, we will not feel lonely, as we will know we are loved; we are cared for, and our presence is missed and anticipated. Being alone is usually temporary, while loneliness can be an ongoing feeling. Long-term aloneness can surely, however, lead to loneliness.

God did not create us to be alone (Genesis 2:18)—and that does not refer exclusively to marriage. The fact that we were created to live in the presence of God indicates that we are relational creatures. From the very beginning, God established a relationship with Adam and Eve to which they responded naturally (Genesis 1:26-27; 3:8-9). Loneliness is unnatural from the divine perspective. God's two sources of relief for loneliness are fellowship with Himself and fellowship with other people. We need to know and assure ourselves daily that God has not abandoned us, that He is with us every moment (Matthew 28:20; Hebrews 13:5). And we need to form and nurture relationships with other people. It is in close, intimate relationships with others that human loneliness is most readily overcome. Paul's illustration of Christians being like the parts of a human body suggests just how intimately we are to be tied one to another—and how important every person is to the rest (1 Corinthians 12:12-27). It is very difficult to be a healthy Christian who lives alone—apart from the body of Christ.

Since God has created in us such a way that we have an emptiness in us that can only be filled by an intimate relationship with Almighty God, we must first fill that emptiness with times of personal devotion, reading His Word, and prayer. Then we take the promises of His Word to heart and pursue and nurture relationships with other people. In both cases, time and effort are required. But when invested, relationships with God and other people become a strong defense against loneliness.

> *We need to know and assure ourselves daily that God has not abandoned us, that He is with us every moment.*

PERSEVERANCE

How do I develop and maintain an eternal perspective?

To develop an eternal perspective, not only are we to set our *heart* on heaven but we are to set our *mind* on heaven. We must not only *seek* heaven, we must *think* heaven. That is, we must love God with all our heart as well as all our mind (Matthew 22:37). Staying centered on Jesus involves our mind as well as our emotions. We are to mind heavenly things. The focus of our mind is not so much to be on the place we call heaven but on the spiritual reality of heaven that controls our whole motivation. This is to be our pattern of life as followers of Christ. If you will notice in Colossians 3:2, there is a corresponding negative phrase that follows the first instruction. It says: "Set your mind on things above, not on things on the earth."

Some critics have said of some Christians, "They are so heavenly minded they are of no earthly good." But when Paul writes "not on things on the earth," he's not saying that we should live oblivious to the realities of life on this earth. There is work to do, families to care for, laws to be obeyed, people to serve—obviously we must participate in all such affairs. Indeed, they absorb the majority of our life! Instead, Paul is saying that we live on earth as citizens of heaven: "For our citizenship is in heaven" (Philippians 3:20a). We bring a heavenly perspective to all our earthly tasks. And we keep that heavenly perspective by being involved in extending God's kingdom on earth, just as Jesus prayed: "Your kingdom come. Your will be done on earth as *it is* in heaven" (Matthew 6:10).

> *Set your mind on things above,*
> *not on things on the earth.*
> ~ **Colossians 3:2**

How can I share the Gospel if people are opposed to hearing it?

It has been said that evangelism is sharing Christ in the power of the Holy Spirit and leaving the results to God. That definition presumes that people will allow you to speak to them about Christ. Some people will and some people will not. When we proclaim the truth, we will always encounter opposition. And yet Christ's Great Commission compels us to continue sowing the seeds of the Gospel until He returns.

The apostle Paul experienced constant opposition as he spread the Gospel. He wrote that Christ was "to the Jews a stumbling block and to the [Gentiles] foolishness" (1 Corinthians 1:23). But Paul and his companions never ceased to spread the Gospel wherever they went, even at great cost to their lives. In the first century, the apostles traveled from town to town preaching, almost always finding some who believed (Acts 16:11-15). If they were opposed or driven out of town, they could move on to a new audience. But what if opposition comes from a neighbor, a coworker, a family member or relative—

someone you are forced to be with on a consistent basis? In that case, if you can't preach by *words*, you must preach by *deeds*. You must become the salt and light Jesus described in Matthew 5:13-16. You must "let your light so shine before men, that they may see your good works and glorify your Father in heaven."

If you can't preach by words, you must preach by deeds.

FINANCES

How can I find peace when dealing with financial loss and indebtedness?

The most recent economic upheaval in our nation and the world began in 2008 with "the Great Recession." For many, investments soured, jobs were lost and savings used up, retirement plans evaporated, homes declined in value—and many have never recovered. Even Christians who have been faithful managers of their money and given faithfully to God's work were affected. As in all other "natural" disasters that strike our world, God gives no promise of exemption to Christians. Rather, He does promise that He will be with us in such times and keep us in His eternal care (1 Thessalonians 5:24). Financial loss can be traumatic. In such times, it is important to focus on what no one can take away: the love of God and our relationships with family and others. The positive part of losing our treasure is that we are reminded that earth is not a safe storehouse. Jesus touched on this when He exhorted His followers to store up treasure in heaven, not on earth (Matthew 6:19-21). It is a reminder to us not to invest in things that are temporary but to invest in things that will last for eternity. Financial loss forces us to seek those things that are above, where Christ is, sitting at the right hand of God.

> *Only two things will last for eternity: the souls of people and the Word of God.*

Is it wrong to find security in my income?

There are two ways to look at financial security: short-term and long-term. The Bible teaches us to work hard, save, and prepare ahead (Proverbs 6:6-8). There is a short-term sense of security that comes from knowing we have been responsible and diligent and have funds set aside should emergencies arise in our life or others' lives. Being solvent in the short-term allows us to have funds to help others and keeps us from being a burden on them. Even in the short-term, however, the Bible tells us that everything we have comes from God: money (1 Chronicles 29:14), as well as the grace to live responsibly (Ephesians 2:8-10). So ultimately, our security is in God.

Long-term, money can never be our primary source of security. Physically, money can be here today and gone tomorrow. Spiritually, whatever we put our ultimate security in becomes our god. And Jesus said we cannot put our security in God and money (things of this world) at the same time. Oftentimes people let money get in between them and God and, in essence, block out everything God wants to do in their life. Paul touched on this danger when he wrote that "the love of money is a root of all *kinds* of evil, for which some have strayed from the faith in their greediness, and pierced themselves through with many sorrows" (1 Timothy 6:10). It is important to desire God above all else so that you are not trying to serve two masters. We should only put our security in that which is permanent and which helps, not hinders, the more of it we have. Money does not meet those tests—but God does.

Whatever we put our ultimate security in becomes our god.

Should I tithe even when I am experiencing financial problems?

A fundamental principle concerning the tithe is found in Leviticus 27:30: "And all the tithe of the land, *whether* of the seed of the land or of the fruit of the tree, *is* the Lord's. It *is* holy to the Lord" (italics added). "Holy to the Lord" reaffirms the fact that it is His, "holy" meaning "set apart for." There are times when people go through a season of shortage because of things that are completely out of their control. But if we apply the principle in Leviticus to our giving, then there would never be a time we would not tithe, since the tithe, whether our income is large or small, belongs to God. Therefore, we are reconciled to living on nine-tenths of what comes in; the thought of not tithing should never be an issue. But even such a committed approach can lack proper motivation, as Jesus explained to religious leaders in His day (Matthew 23:23). Jesus pointed out that the Law is intended to serve man, not man the Law (Mark 2:27).

The higher motivation in giving is always the heart—our willingness to give generously to God in response to His generosity to us. In 2 Corinthians chapters 8 and 9, Paul affirms that it is not the amount we give but the willingness and cheerfulness with which we give. That doesn't mean the amount is not important. Paul also says we should give as we have been blessed to give—generosity being the benchmark. But generosity is marked by more than the amount. The churches in Macedonia gave out of their poverty—that is, sacrificially, even "beyond *their* ability" (2 Corinthians 8:1-4). And though a poor widow Jesus observed giving had only two pennies to give, Jesus said she had given more generously than those who gave more (Mark 12:41-44). God doesn't need our money, but He does need to know our hearts are His. What He is saying is this: "I don't expect of you what is impossible. What I do expect is your willing heart."

> *The higher motivation in giving is always the heart.*

Does God always bless people when they tithe?

When the Jews returned from Babylon to Jerusalem, they had many demands on their resources as they settled in Judea and established incomes. As a result, they were not faithful in giving the tithe to God. The prophet Malachi said they were robbing God. He gave them a challenge: Bring God's tithe to the temple and see if God "will not open for you the windows of heaven and pour out for you *such* blessing that *there will* not *be room* enough *to receive it*" (Malachi 3:10). From the beginning, Israel was told that if they kept God's covenant, they would be blessed (Deuteronomy 28:1-14). As we walk in God's new covenant today (Matthew 26:28), we should expect the same blessing from God when we are generous toward God and others.

People who begin to tithe faithfully to God learn that they live better on 90 percent of their income than they did on 100 percent when they weren't tithing. No one can explain that rationally, but it can be explained as the blessing of God. Jesus echoed

Malachi's words when He said, "Give, and it will be given to you: good measure, pressed down, shaken together, and running over will be put into your bosom. For with the same measure that you use, it will be measured back to you" (Luke 6:38). That is the promise of God—and God always keeps His promises. If we do what He tells us to do, He will meet our needs. If we can trust God for eternity, surely we can trust Him for today. Put God first and give Him what is rightfully His—He will take care of you.

> *When we give to God, it is not a credit to our own creativity and resourcefulness, but to His.*

PRAYER

> **Why is it important to ask God for our basic needs?**

The most important reason to pray for our daily needs is that Jesus taught us to pray that way: "Our Father in heaven, . . . give us this day our daily bread" (Matthew 6:9, 11). But it was Jesus who preceded His instructions on prayer with this fact: "For your Father knows the things you have need of before you ask Him" (verse 8). So the question is not only, Why pray for daily needs? but, Why pray at all if God already knows what our daily needs are?

The answer is because prayer shapes our understanding of God's will, helping us know what to ask for, and deepens our knowledge of God through intimacy with Him. More than anything, prayer builds our trust. When we bow before God daily and thank Him for His promises to provide what we need and for His faithfulness, we build our trust that He will continue to provide in the future.

The effective, fervent prayer of a righteous man avails much.

~ James 5:16

What is the best way to keep the communication channel open with God?

We are invited to "come boldly to the throne of grace, that we may obtain mercy and find grace to help in time of need" (Hebrews 4:16). Since the presence of God is a holy presence, we cannot enter in an unholy state—meaning, if we are unrepentant about sin in our life. In Christ, we can stand before God in a forgiven, holy state. But if we have grieved the Holy Spirit by failing to confess our sins, we cannot enjoy intimate fellowship with God: "If we say that we have fellowship with Him, and walk in darkness, we lie and do not practice the truth" (1 John 1:6).

The best way to keep our communication channels open with God is to remain filled with the Spirit and keep short accounts concerning our sins (1 John 1:9). The Holy Spirit is our guide in prayer, the One who guides us into all truth (John 16:13). Quenching His promptings concerning unforgiveness toward another can be a barrier in prayer. This is when the communication channel gets sluggish—we often find it difficult to forgive those who have hurt or harmed us in some way. But Jesus said God will not forgive us if we have not forgiven those who have sinned against us (Matthew 6:14-15). Those who live by God's forgiveness must imitate it.

In Christ, we can stand before God in a forgiven, holy state.

STRENGTH

When I feel weak, where can I go to gain strength?

The clearest answer to this question comes from Paul's experience with his own weakness: "For when I am weak, then I am strong" (2 Corinthians 12:10b). We could read the verse this way: "For when I am weak, [I am given grace from God, and] then I am strong." Therefore, we could define *grace* as the ability or strength of God imparted to man. What we lack, God provided by His unmerited favor—and that certainly includes strength.

But how do we *receive* God's grace that equates to strength in our life? Like everything else in the Christian life—by faith. We walk in dependence on the promises of God and the power of the Holy Spirit: "that He would grant you, according to the riches of His glory, to be strengthened with might through His Spirit in the inner man" (Ephesians 3:16). Jesus' promise to the disciples was that they would receive power (strength, boldness) when the Holy Spirit came upon them, which He did at Pentecost (Acts 1:8). And their post-Pentecost actions indicate that the power of the Spirit was working in them.

The Holy Spirit is also our Helper, or Comforter (John 14:26). After Jesus left earth, the Father sent the Spirit to live in followers of Jesus to help them, comfort them, counsel them, and guide them. If you are a Christian, the Holy Spirit dwells in you. In moments of weakness, ask Him to impart God's grace to you in a way that will enable you to manifest the strength you need. Whatever problems you may have, remember, God is your Creator, redeemer, and sustainer—He is enough.

> *Soaring by faith means setting your sights on heights you could never reach without God's help.*

How can I encourage others who need strength?

Imagine if you were one of the saints mentioned as a hero of faith in Hebrews 11. The writer of Hebrews pictures them as a "great . . . cloud of witnesses" in heaven (Hebrews 12:1). It is as if they are leaning over the parapets of heaven, looking down on us now as we go through challenging times in life, shouting, "You can do this! Don't give up! Run with endurance! Keep your eyes focused on the prize that is Jesus!"

When you stop for a moment and start looking around, you will realize there are many people who are going through times of difficulty. So what would you say if you were in that cloud of witnesses, if you were one of the heroes of faith, encouraging someone in danger of stumbling? You would no doubt offer to pray with and for that person. You would probably share part of your story of faith and overcoming discouragement. You might share a Scripture like Psalm 16:8: "I have set the LORD always before me; because He is at my right hand I shall not be moved." The testimony of God's faithfulness in our time of weakness is a powerful encouragement to those who need strength. God comforts us in our time of tribulation so that we can in turn comfort others (2 Corinthians 1:3-4).

> *God comforts us in our time of tribulation so that we can in turn comfort others.*

PEACE

How can I have peace with God?

Paul writes that, before being reconciled to God, our relationship with God was adversarial: We were "enemies" of God (Romans 5:10). Every war is concluded when peace is brokered between the two sides, and that is what happened to us: "Therefore, having been justified by faith, we have peace with God through our Lord Jesus Christ" (Romans 5:1).

In that verse Paul says several important things about peace with God. First, if we are a Christian, we have that peace; the adversarial relationship is over. Second, peace came "through our Lord Jesus Christ." This is consistent with what Jesus Himself said: "No one comes to the Father except through Me" (John

14:6b). Third, we were justified by faith in Christ. Peace doesn't come by our good works but through faith in Christ (Ephesians 2:8-9). God declared us justified—made us acceptable in His sight—by faith in Christ alone because Christ removed the barrier of sin. When Christ came into the world as a baby in Bethlehem, the angels proclaimed, "Glory to God in the highest, and on earth peace . . ." (Luke 2:14). "Peace" in Greek is *eirene*—the joining together of two opposing parties or forces. That was made possible when Christ came to earth to bear the sins of the world and provide peace with God.

Now may the God of hope fill you with all joy and peace in believing, that you may abound in hope by the power of the Holy Spirit.
~ Romans 15:13

Can I have peace with God but not feel at peace?

Circumstances don't change fundamental realities. We can be a member of a family, a citizen of a nation, or a member of a church, and for any number of reasons fail to enjoy the benefits of our status. Likewise, we can have peace with God yet not be living in peace. Our unrest doesn't negate our status with God. But we need to bring our experience of peace in line with our status of peace. We can know intellectually that Christ has provided peace with God yet still not be experiencing peace in our daily life.

We lose our experience of peace due to worry, fear, a blemish on our conscience, a broken relationship, stress, ill health, or any number of other reasons. We have to remember that daily peace is a manifestation of the presence of the Spirit of God: "But the fruit of the Spirit is . . . peace" (Galatians 5:22). When we are giving the Spirit free reign in our life, we will experience the peace *of* God that should flow from having peace *with* God. If we have sins, we confess them. If we have worries or fears, we give them to God through prayer with thanksgiving. If our mind is filled with disruptive thoughts, we dwell on kingdom truths. When we do that, the peace of God will guard our heart and mind, and the God of peace will be with us (Philippians 4:6-9).

We need to bring our experience of peace in line with our status of peace.

Wisdom

What is worldly wisdom?

The apostle James characterizes worldly wisdom in three ways: "earthly, sensual, demonic" (James 3:15). If there was a first-century city that displayed those three characteristics dramatically, it was Corinth. Not surprisingly, it was in his first letter to the church in Corinth where Paul contrasted worldly wisdom with godly wisdom at length.

Worldly wisdom is human wisdom, or humanism—the best attempts of man to explain the world and the meaning of life. But Paul says, "the wisdom of this world is foolishness with God" (1 Corinthians 3:19a). He made sure the Corinthians understood that he did not use "persuasive words of human wisdom" when he preached to them, but words based on "Christ the power of God and the wisdom of God" (1:24; 2:4). Our sources for heavenly wisdom are the written and living Word of God—Scripture and Jesus Christ—as revealed and empowered by the Holy Spirit. In contrast to worldly wisdom, this wisdom is heavenly, spiritual, and godly—"revealed . . . to us through His Spirit" (2:10).

Whenever man has tried to construct his life on a foundation of the world's wisdom, he has ended up defeated, discouraged, and disappointed. Christians today must fight the temptation to build their lives on the foundation of the world's wisdom.

The fear of the LORD is the beginning of wisdom; a good understanding have all those who do His commandments.
~ Psalm 111:10

Can I have both worldly wisdom and godly wisdom?

No—there is no overlap between the two. Understanding that worldly wisdom is "earthly, sensual, demonic" (James 3:15), consider what John says about the Christian and the world: "Do not love the world or the things in the world. If anyone loves the world, the love of the Father is not in him. For all that is in the world—the lust of the flesh, the lust of the eyes, and the pride of life—is not of the Father but is of the world. And the world is passing away, and the lust of it; but he who does the will of God abides forever" (1 John 2:15-17).

Note that John says love of the Father and love of the world are mutually exclusive. They cannot occupy the same space, the same heart, at the same time. That doesn't mean that a Christian cannot become infatuated with worldly goods, attractions, or power in the moment. It does mean that no sincere Christian would seek to walk both paths at the same time. If you are a believer, here's what you need to remember: The wisdom of the world belongs to the way you used to be before you became a Christian. It should not characterize the new you, because you are to live in a new realm.

Today ask God to help you to "keep right" as you travel down life's highway.

How can I gain godly wisdom?

Solomon wrote that godly wisdom comes from God: "For the LORD gives wisdom; from His mouth *come* knowledge and understanding" (Proverbs 2:6). And God gives wisdom as a result of us searching diligently for it, as we would seek for "silver" and for "hidden treasures" (verse 4). In reality, our search is to learn to fear the Lord, for it is from Him that wisdom comes. As James wrote, "If any of you lacks wisdom, let him ask of God" (James 1:5). Solomon also said, "Do not be wise in your own eyes; fear the LORD and depart from evil" (Proverbs 3:7). Godly wisdom does not spring from the natural heart of man; it springs from a heart that fears (honors, respects) God. It is possible that some of us do not have God's wisdom because we have not yet come to the place where we understand that we lack it in ourselves. We are going about doing what we think is right, constructing our own programs, when God wants to bring us to a place of poverty in terms of our own wisdom so that we might reach out to receive His.

MARRIAGE
AND FAMILY

Therefore a man
shall leave his
father and mother
and be joined to his
wife, and they shall
become one flesh.

Genesis 2:24

MARRIAGE

> **How can my spouse and I enjoy greater unity?**

God said it first in the Garden of Eden: A man and woman will marry "and they shall become one flesh" (Genesis 2:24). "One flesh" is repeated four more times in Scripture to refer to the union of husband and wife. It would be a mistake to think the phrase refers solely to the physical union of a married couple (though it certainly means that). It encompasses much more.

Remember: Woman was taken from man in the beginning (Genesis 2:20-23), and her return to him in marriage makes him whole again. That wholeness is multidimensional: physical, spiritual, emotional, intellectual. God's ideal is complete unity between the two, their differences not separating them but completing and complementing them. So why is there ever disunity in marriage? For the same reason there is disunity in any relationship after the entrance of sin into the world—the effect of self-serving. Marriage is a lifelong process of a couple yielding their self-interests to the higher goal of unity in marriage. The high principle of mutual submission among Christians should govern all relationships in the body of Christ: "submitting to one another in the fear of God" (Ephesians 5:21). Paul's word for wives to submit to their husbands follows that verse (22). While there is a hierarchy in marriage, the larger principle of loving, mutual submission will go far in removing barriers to unity. The "one flesh" of marriage is accomplished when, together, a couple loves their way to wholeness by progressively tearing down the barriers of sin that grow up between them.

> **Sometimes I only see the negative characteristics of my spouse. Why is positive affirmation important?**

If you want to have a strong relationship, you need to have the kind of communication that will build one another up and not tear one another down. *Edifice* is an older English word for "building." Edification, therefore, is the New Testament word for "building up"—the opposite of tearing down. It was a high priority for the apostle Paul in his letters, encouraging Christians to say and do things that would "build up" each other. That is, saying positive, complimentary, encouraging, wise words—putting into speech the kinds of thoughts Paul described in Philippians 4:8-9. If we can build ourselves up with "virtuous" and "praiseworthy" *thoughts*, we can build up others with virtuous and praiseworthy *words* (verse 8). Such words can be seen as stones laid one on another in the construction of a mature church, relationship, family, or marriage.

If you are a spouse, would you prefer to live in a strong, safe, well-built house (marriage) or one that offers scant protection from the elements of the world? The way to build such a house is by affirming your spouse at every opportunity. Every act of tearing down is like removing a shingle or stone that will one day have to be replaced. Better to stay focused on building.

Sometimes our greatest work is inspiring others to do their greatest work.

How can I feel more secure in my marriage?

Like all else in God's kingdom, we reap what we sow (Galatians 6:7). Therefore, if we want to reap security in marriage, we have to sow security. We have to do everything we can to be honest, loyal, transparent, unconditionally loving, and forgiving toward our spouse. Isn't that what makes us secure in the presence of God? It will never work for one spouse to say to another, "Make me more secure!" Yes, you can discuss the matter, speaking the truth in love (Ephesians 4:15). But far better is to *demonstrate* security toward your spouse. God promises that when you sow those seeds, you will reap a harvest in kind.

And what gives you the ability to sow seeds of security into your marriage? *Your security in Christ.* No spouse can depend on another human being for ultimate security in life or in marriage. We desire security and we relish it when we have it, but people sometimes fail; we will sometimes be disappointed. But we will never be disappointed in how we are loved by Christ. He is honest, loyal, transparent, unconditionally loving, and forgiving toward us—and that makes us secure enough to sow those same seeds in the life of a spouse. God wants marriage to be a refuge, a safe harbor, from the world. He wants spouses to be secure in one another's arms, to feel the same security between one another as the Church feels in the arms of Christ (Ephesians 5:22-33). When spouses are secure in Christ, they can rest. They have nothing to prove and no reason to earn approval or security and are therefore free to give. When both spouses are secure in Christ, they are free to sow seeds of security in one another's life—and reap the bountiful harvest.

God wants marriage to be a refuge, a safe harbor, from the world.

How do I keep Christ at the center of my marriage?

Think of two pianos as an illustration of marriage: Imagine them representing husband and wife. There is a tuning fork that represents Christ. First one piano, then the other, is tuned perfectly to the tuning fork. When that happens, both pianos are likewise in tune with each other.

That can only happen as each spouse individually draws closer to Christ or lives more "in tune" to Christ. And that happens the same way in every life—through devotion, obedience, and submission to His lordship. We don't draw near to Christ *so that* our marriage will be better. That would make Christ a means to an end when, in fact, He is "the end" itself. We submit to the lordship of Christ because it is our loving and joyful obligation. And when we do, every part of life will be sweeter—whether individually or in relationships, and certainly in marriage.

God intends that we develop a wonderfully intimate relationship with the precious person He has given us to be our husband or wife, and it begins with Christ at the center—He bonds the marriage together.

Marriage is like most things in life—you ultimately get out of it what you invest in it.

Is there a way to prevent divorce in my marriage?

The surest way to prevent divorce is for both spouses to attend seriously to their wedding vows which for centuries have implied permanence in marriage. The wise King Solomon put it succinctly: "Better not to vow than to vow and not pay" (Ecclesiastes 5:5). While Jesus allowed for the possibility of divorce in the case of marital infidelity, He assigned the cause ultimately to the hardness of the human heart (Matthew 19:8-9). Nowhere in the Bible does it say couples *must* divorce in the case of unfaithfulness. Love can cover "a multitude of sins" (Proverbs 10:12).

Almost never is unfaithfulness a random act of passion, a spur-of-the-moment decision. Rather, it is the culmination of a chain of unfaithful thoughts and deeds that concludes in a marriage-threatening choice. The best way to keep that chain of events from ever growing is to break its links when they are first forged. And that calls for honesty and openness between marriage partners. It calls for dialogue, with assistance if needed, about needs and expectations. It calls for humility and other-centeredness. And it calls for forgiveness and reconciliation. Divorce need not ever happen outside dramatic, life-threatening danger or damage to family members. Marriages can be divorce-proofed by giving the devil and human nature no opportunity to threaten sacred vows. There is no way that any marriage will ever work without these foundational principles between husband and wife, as well as a commitment to God and one another.

Love hangs on with tenacity when other hands let go in despair.

How can I deal with anger toward my spouse?

Sinful anger is a threat in marriage just as it is in any relationship—only more so. Because of accumulated sins, intimacy of knowledge, grudges borne, sins unforgiven, and ungodly expectations, marriage is a perfect venue for displays of anger. The apostle Paul gives a *remedy* and a *result* if the remedy is not applied. The *remedy* for dealing with anger in marriage is, "Do not let the sun go down on your wrath" (Ephesians 4:26). That is, deal with the issues that fuel anger quickly. That does not mean reacting impulsively. Rather, it means talking honestly and lovingly in a way that promotes forgiveness and reconciliation. Allowing anger to fester can result in a "root of bitterness springing up" that can cause many to "become defiled" (Hebrews 12:15).

The *result* if anger is not resolved quickly is that we "give place to the devil" (Ephesians 4:27). Anger may be the devil's greatest opportunity for creating division because of the emotions involved. Resolving issues quickly and in a loving, gentle manner is the best way to keep the devil where he belongs—out of your marriage.

Do I always have to be the one to ask for forgiveness?

In a word, yes. Unless you can find a verse in the Bible that gives you permission not to forgive, you always have to be "the one." In this verse from Ephesians, there seems to be little room concerning forgiving or asking for forgiveness: "And be kind to one another, tenderhearted, forgiving one another, even as God in Christ forgave you" (Ephesians 4:32). The standard is, "as God in Christ forgave you." Does God ever not forgive us? If He doesn't, then neither are we free to withhold forgiveness until someone else apologizes first. Nor are we free *not* to apologize while we wait on another.

Married couples struggle with this. If a disagreement arises in which both have reason to apologize, someone usually goes first. And whoever does that most often begins to resent being "the one." But if you have done something—a word or deed—for which you should apologize, your obligation is unconditional. You should not wait to see if your spouse will apologize first. You should do what is your responsibility. Remember that in this whole matter of forgiveness in general, and certainly in marriage, there is no such thing as counting (Matthew 18:21-22). Ideally, spouses should meet each other in the hallway, both seeking to initiate reconciliation, after a disagreement. But if that doesn't happen, walk the whole way yourself. Be first to apologize and forgive.

> *And be kind to one another, tenderhearted, forgiving one another, even as God in Christ forgave you.*
> *~Ephesians 4:32*

I want to experience true love. What does that look like?

Marriage is the norm for human beings—it is the means by which man was to "be fruitful and multiply" (Genesis 1:28). The desire for marriage is God-given; He put it into our hearts. God needed human beings to populate the earth, so He hardwired men and women to form a union and create a family. It is in our genes for men and women to be attracted to one another. That makes married love a good thing, a gift from God.

There is *recognizing* married love and there is *realizing* married love. Recognizing love—deciding on the one person with whom you want to spend the rest of your life—is done carefully. When men find a woman they can love the way Christ loves the Church, they know they have found "the one." And when women find a man they can honor the way the Church honors Christ, they too have found "the one" (Ephesians 5:22-33). Realizing love, after the wonder of courtship settles into working out a life together, is best guided by 1 Corinthians 13. Love transitions from being something "I feel" to something "I do." Try reading 1 Corinthians 13:4-8a and substituting your name for the word "love"—and see if Paul is describing you. If so, you have realized what love looks like.

> *Love suffers long and is kind; love does not envy; love does not parade itself, is not puffed up; does not behave rudely, does not seek its own, is not provoked, thinks no evil; does not rejoice in iniquity, but rejoices in the truth; bears all things, believes all things, hopes all things, endures all things. Love never fails.*
> *~1 Corinthians 13:4-8a*

Is there a reason for my being single? Is it punishment?

Most people, by God's design, *want* to marry and raise a family. But there have been many godly people through the ages who have remained single for a variety of reasons. Usually, it has to do with focusing on what God has called them to do. Paul made it very clear in 1 Corinthians 7 that single people live less distracted lives than married people. And Paul viewed his own life as a bachelor as a gift from God (verse 7). To most, God gives the gift of a spouse; to some, He gives the gift of a single life. You will know which gift you have been given. If you desire to be married, that is what you should pursue *with patient submission to God's timing*. As long as you are single, consider yourself as blessed as you will be if you marry. One state is no more or less blessed than the other. Being where God wants you to be is the surest way to enjoy His blessing. So praise God for who you are and where He has placed you. God is interested in your life. He loves you and only wants what is best for you.

PARENTING

How can I protect my family from ungodly influences?

In ancient times, walled cities used watchmen to scan the horizon for signs of approaching danger. But King Solomon reminds us, "Unless the LORD guards the city, the watchman stays awake in vain" (Psalm 127:1b). And Solomon wrote the same about the home: "Unless the LORD builds the house, they labor in vain who build it" (verse 1a). Houses and cities—that is, the people in them—must be watched over by God. He is the only watchman who can keep us safe.

Parents must spend time praying that God will be the Watchman over their home. And they must strike the right balance between *filtering* and *filling*—filtering out the negative influences of the world and filling the home with godly influences. To do either without the other will lead to an unbalanced result. Ultimately, parenting is a partnership between parents and God. Knowing that God loves children even more than their parents do is a great comfort. God is always on the wall, watching and defending our home.

> *Great children are raised by great parents who serve a great God with great expectations for the outcome.*

Why is praying for my children important?

It is an incredible privilege to cover our children in prayer. We must pray for our children for the same reasons we must pray for other needs and desires. But we must pray in unique ways because of their unique requirements. They're fighting battles most of us don't know about that are intense, and they need to know that their mom and dad are standing with them and praying for them. Depending on their age, children can be young and inexperienced, they can be naïve and foolish, they can be unafraid of danger, they can be easily deceived, they are often impulsive, and they do not have a long-term view of life. Each of those unique vulnerabilities becomes a focal point for prayer. Parents can be years, sometimes decades, past their own childhood and often forget what life is like for young children. We should pray for God to put a hedge of protection around them (Job 1:9) and for God's angels to watch over them (Hebrews 1:14). And we should ask God for grace for them to learn that which will be most important in their relationship with Him: obedience

(Ephesians 6:1). Days passed without prayer can never be reclaimed. Bringing a child before God's throne of grace, asking for mercy and grace and help, may be a parent's most enduring act of love.

> *Bringing a child before God's throne of grace, asking for mercy and grace and help, may be a parent's most enduring act of love.*

What can I do to better encourage my children?

When the apostle Paul was outlining responsibilities for various roles in the body of Christ—husbands, wives, children, fathers, slaves, masters (Ephesians 5:22-6:9)—his word to fathers is important. First the negative: "And you, fathers, do not provoke your children to wrath." Then the positive: ". . . but bring them up in the training and admonition of the Lord" (Ephesians 6:4).

It is noteworthy that these instructions are given to "fathers," not to "parents." Though he wasn't a father, Paul knew what the potential was for fathers to discourage their children with demands and expectations.

The emotions in that verse can best be offset by one biblical idea: encouragement. More than anything, children need encouragement. (And that doesn't mean getting a trophy just for showing up; they need to learn that fulfilling responsibilities is to be expected in life.) But when failure and falls happen, and all parents know they will, our children need to be encouraged. God holds us responsible for teaching them that they are very special. Words, hugs, loving correction, patient instruction, patience, unconditional love and forgiveness, rewards and commendations—the challenge is not *how* to encourage, but *encouraging*. In addition to praying for our children, we need to pray for parents to be the encouragers their children need. Children are God's blessing to us—we need to unashamedly encourage and bless them, and we need to praise God openly for them.

Children are encouraged when we affirm their originality.

What causes my child to rebel?

Proverbs 22:15 says, "Foolishness *is* bound up in the heart of a child." And that doesn't mean silliness or acting up. Foolishness in Proverbs is moral stubbornness and rebellion. It's in the heart of a child because he or she is a human being, a son or daughter of Adam. That doesn't mean every child is going to go off the deep end and bring shame and embarrassment to his parents. But it does mean every child is going to fight his way out of his cocoon to emerge into the person he was created by God to be. And that's where parents must be prepared, be careful, and be prayerful.

The purpose of childhood is to reach adulthood, and the transition can be difficult. But parents who understand the process can make the journey smoother by not demanding that their children grow up to be like them. Adolescents have to put off childhood before they can put on adulthood, and that change can take years. It can be every bit as confusing for the child as the parent. But the parent is obligated to be wiser, more patient, and more understanding having (hopefully) made the transition themselves. By God's grace, when children kick against the cocoon, they can discover, with their parents' help, there is far less resistance than they expected. And they can come out smiling.

Being a successful parent requires that you speak two languages—yours and theirs.

How can I deal with a rebellious child in my home?

Parents hopefully give birth to their children three times in life: when they enter the world, when they enter adolescence, and when they enter the kingdom of God. The first two births are often accompanied by crying and discomfort until the newborns settle into their new environment. Most rebellion occurs in the preteen and teenage years, often without rhyme or reason. Which child in a family rebels most or least cannot always be predicted and can rarely be controlled. What is needed in all three birth scenarios is an experienced "midwife"—someone to make the passage successful and safe. God puts parents in the place of responsibility in the home. Although parents can't protect their adolescent children from the pain of rebellion, they can stay beside them to provide safety and security. Sometimes firm boundaries and loving correction are needed—prayerful parents must do their best to find wisdom (James 1:5). And they must remain the parents, letting a struggling child know that boundaries won't be moved. Above all, parents must remain vigilant in their quest to love a rebellious child unconditionally and communicate that love—the message at the heart of the Bible's best story about a rebellious child (Luke 15:11-32).

Parents must remain vigilant in their quest to love a rebellious child unconditionally and communicate that love.

How do I keep my family from falling apart?

God is the architect and the builder of the home (Psalm 127:1). But we are the laborers; we are the ones responsible for taking His design and laboring under His guidance to build what is pleasing to Him and to ourselves. The Bible clearly says: To try and build a home apart from God at its head is vanity (verse 1). It may be an attractive home on the outside, but unless it is filled with fruitfulness, life, and unity on the inside, it will have fallen short of His design. Yes, we can recover. We can always work to correct what we built by our own design and efforts. His grace is greater than our failure (Romans 5:20). But how much more blessed it is to build by His design from the beginning.

Psalm 128 paints a wonderful picture of family life: "Your wife *shall be* like a fruitful vine in the very heart of your house, your children like olive plants all around your table" (verse 3). Those words speak of life, abundance, growth, and unity. And who is fortunate enough to enjoy such a lovely setting? "Behold, thus shall the man be blessed who fears the

LORD" (verse 4). Honoring and respecting God is always the starting point for blessedness. A family sitting around a table, holding hands, heads bowed in grateful recognition of God's provision—that's a picture of a family that is falling *together*, not falling *apart*.

> *The only way to end up with a house that reflects God as the architect is to build according to His plan— the Word of God.*

How can I remain patient when my children make poor decisions?

A great Hebrew phrase, found 68 times from Genesis through Acts, is, "And it came to pass." While it isn't used with reference to raising children, parents should take note: Childhood didn't come to *stay*; it came to *pass!* That knowledge alone, that a difficult situation is temporary, is enough to give us patience. And childhood is temporary. God gives us children to raise for a few years before we release them into the world. It is not worth damaging our relationship with a child over a small thing. Our love should be a constant force in their lives regardless of the decisions they make. We want to build into their lives, while we have them near, the kind of love and bond that will keep them coming back for counsel as they mature. If we are patient with children when they are young, they are more likely to expect we will be patient with them when they are older. And remember: Patience is the fruit of the Spirit (Galatians 5:22). You don't have to be patient in your own strength. Christ wants to be patient with your children through you as you prayerfully yield to the Spirit in trying moments. This difficulty you are experiencing, you will get on the other side of it. Remain strong and hang on to the promises of God—He will see you through it.

*Trust and Patience
are the two
authors of the
book called Love.*

How can I be a better role model for my children?

There is a beautiful picture of modeling the spiritual life in Deuteronomy 6:6-9—Moses' instructions to parents about how to communicate God's truths to their children. In short, he said to integrate God's truth into all the aspects of daily life: whether you are sitting around the house or out on the town, when you're getting ready for bed and when you're making breakfast, when you're leaving home and when you're arriving home—and all the times and places in between. That's what the figure of speech meant that Moses used: talk about and live out God's truth in every dimension of life. Don't make life with God *religious* just on *one day* of the week; make it a *regular* part of *every day* of the week. The way parents model their faith before their children on a daily basis—for good or for bad—has a far greater impact than what they say about their faith. *Walk* matters more than *talk*. Both are important, but from the emotional perspective that shapes a child's life, what they *see* matters more than what they *hear*.

That means our children must see Jesus when they look at us. We want them to be drawn to us because they are unknowingly drawn to Jesus—His love, compassion, patience, understanding, forgiveness, humility, and wisdom. When that happens, getting to know Jesus when they are older will be the most natural of discoveries. If you want your kids to be excited about their faith, they need to see that this isn't just a duty you do—your walk with God is a wonderful privilege. You serve the King of kings and the Lord of lords! Make them hunger and thirst for the things of God by seeing your growing and committed walk with Him.

Talk about and live out God's truth in every dimension of life.

Will God forgive me if I've terminated a pregnancy?

The biblical answer to this question is, "Yes." The Bible does not say that terminating a pregnancy is an unforgivable sin. Children are a heritage of the Lord, so to deny that gift or to destroy it flies in the face of the magnificence of our God. The termination of a pregnancy brings pain and unwritten anguish and hidden scars that can't be wiped away. But if you love God and have asked for His forgiveness, He will forgive. All God asks of a mother who seeks forgiveness is that she accept it; to draw a line in the sand, step over it, and build a life based on the knowledge that she is forgiven—leaving that chapter of her life in God's hands. Once God has said, "You are free and forgiven," that is the end of the matter.

If you have had an abortion, you might ask, How might God use this in my life or in the life of others? Any woman who chooses to terminate a pregnancy and then reflects on it from God's perspective will have learned much. God may want to use that person to impact others who are contemplating an abortion or have already had one. Every experience of pain in life can become a healing balm for someone else. God comforts us "that we may be able to comfort those who are in any trouble, with the comfort with which we ourselves are comforted by God" (2 Corinthians 1:4).

If you love God and have asked for His forgiveness, He will forgive.

When life wounds us and we are in deep pain, we instinctively cry out to God. And it is then that we hear Him and feel His presence so clearly.

SCRIPTURE
REFERENCE
GUIDE

ADVERSITY

Scripture Reference Guide

DEUTERONOMY **31:8** And the LORD, He *is* the One who goes before you. He will be with you, He will not leave you nor forsake you; do not fear nor be dismayed.

JOSHUA **1:9** Have I not commanded you? Be strong and of good courage; do not be afraid, nor be dismayed, for the LORD your God *is* with you wherever you go.

1 CHRONICLES **16:11** Seek the LORD and His strength; seek His face evermore!

PSALM **9:9-10** The LORD also will be a refuge for the oppressed, a refuge in times of trouble. And those who know Your name will put their trust in You; for You, LORD, have not forsaken those who seek You.

PSALM 23:4 Yea, though I walk through the valley of the shadow of death, I will fear no evil; for You *are* with me; Your rod and Your staff, they comfort me.

PSALM 34:19 Many *are* the afflictions of the righteous, but the LORD delivers him out of them all.

PSALM 46:1 God *is* our refuge and strength, a very present help in trouble.

PSALM 55:22 Cast your burden on the LORD, and He shall sustain you; He shall never permit the righteous to be moved.

PROVERBS 24:10 *If* you faint in the day of adversity, your strength *is* small.

Isaiah **40:29-31** He gives power to the weak, and to *those who have* no might He increases strength. Even the youths shall faint and be weary, and the young men shall utterly fall, but those who wait on the LORD shall renew *their* strength; they shall mount up with wings like eagles, they shall run and not be weary, they shall walk and not faint.

Isaiah **41:10** Fear not, for I *am* with you; be not dismayed, for I *am* your God. I will strengthen you, yes, I will help you, I will uphold you with My righteous right hand.

Jeremiah **15:11** Surely it will be well with your remnant; surely I will cause the enemy to intercede with you in the time of adversity and in the time of affliction.

Jeremiah 29:11 For I know the thoughts that I think toward you, says the LORD, thoughts of peace and not of evil, to give you a future and a hope.

Matthew 11:28 Come to Me, all *you* who labor and are heavy laden, and I will give you rest.

John 14:27 Peace I leave with you, My peace I give to you; not as the world gives do I give to you. Let not your heart be troubled, neither let it be afraid.

John 16:33 These things I have spoken to you, that in Me you may have peace. In the world you will have tribulation; but be of good cheer, I have overcome the world.

ROMANS 5:3-5 And not only *that,* but we also glory in tribulations, knowing that tribulation produces perseverance; and perseverance, character; and character, hope. Now hope does not disappoint, because the love of God has been poured out in our hearts by the Holy Spirit who was given to us.

ROMANS 8:28 And we know that all things work together for good to those who love God, to those who are the called according to *His* purpose.

ROMANS 8:38-39 For I am persuaded that neither death nor life, nor angels nor principalities nor powers, nor things present nor things to come, nor height nor depth, nor any other created thing, shall be able to separate us from the love of God which is in Christ Jesus our Lord.

ROMANS **12:2** And do not be conformed to this world, but be transformed by the renewing of your mind, that you may prove what *is* that good and acceptable and perfect will of God.

1 CORINTHIANS **10:13** No temptation has overtaken you except such as is common to man; but God *is* faithful, who will not allow you to be tempted beyond what you are able, but with the temptation will also make the way of escape, that you may be able to bear *it*.

2 CORINTHIANS **1:3-4** Blessed *be* the God and Father of our Lord Jesus Christ, the Father of mercies and God of all comfort, who comforts us in all our tribulation, that we may be able to comfort those who are in any trouble, with the comfort with which we ourselves are comforted by God.

2 Corinthians 4:8-10 *We are* hard-pressed on every side, yet not crushed; *we are* perplexed, but not in despair; persecuted, but not forsaken; struck down, but not destroyed—always carrying about in the body the dying of the Lord Jesus, that the life of Jesus also may be manifested in our body.

2 Corinthians 4:16-17 Therefore we do not lose heart. Even though our outward *man* is perishing, yet the inward man is being renewed day by day. For our light affliction, which is but for a moment, is working for us a far more exceeding *and* eternal weight of glory.

2 Corinthians 12:9 And He said to me, "My grace is sufficient for you, for My strength is made perfect in weakness." Therefore most gladly I will rather boast in my infirmities, that the power of Christ may rest upon me.

PHILIPPIANS 4:6 Be anxious for nothing, but in everything by prayer and supplication, with thanksgiving, let your requests be made known to God.

PHILIPPIANS 4:12-13 I know how to be abased, and I know how to abound. Everywhere and in all things I have learned both to be full and to be hungry, both to abound and to suffer need. I can do all things through Christ who strengthens me.

2 TIMOTHY 3:12 Yes, and all who desire to live godly in Christ Jesus will suffer persecution.

HEBREWS 4:15-16 For we do not have a High Priest who cannot sympathize with our weaknesses, but was in all *points* tempted as *we are, yet* without sin. Let us therefore come boldly to the throne of grace, that we may obtain mercy and find grace to help in time of need.

JAMES 1:2-4 My brethren, count it all joy when you fall into various trials, knowing that the testing of your faith produces patience. But let patience have *its* perfect work, that you may be perfect and complete, lacking nothing.

JAMES 1:12 Blessed *is* the man who endures temptation; for when he has been approved, he will receive the crown of life which the Lord has promised to those who love Him.

JAMES 5:12 But above all, my brethren, do not swear, either by heaven or by earth or with any other oath. But let your "Yes" be "Yes," and *your* "No," "No," lest you fall into judgment.

1 Peter 4:12-13 Beloved, do not think it strange concerning the fiery trial which is to try you, as though some strange thing happened to you; but rejoice to the extent that you partake of Christ's sufferings, that when His glory is revealed, you may also be glad with exceeding joy.

1 Peter 4:19 Therefore let those who suffer according to the will of God commit their souls *to Him* in doing good, as to a faithful Creator.

1 Peter 5:6-7 Therefore humble yourselves under the mighty hand of God, that He may exalt you in due time, casting all your care upon Him, for He cares for you.

1 Peter 5:10 But may the God of all grace, who called us to His eternal glory by Christ Jesus, after you have suffered a while, perfect, establish, strengthen, and settle *you*.

1 John 2:15-17 Do not love the world or the things in the world. If anyone loves the world, the love of the Father is not in him. For all that *is* in the world—the lust of the flesh, the lust of the eyes, and the pride of life—is not of the Father but is of the world. And the world is passing away, and the lust of it; but he who does the will of God abides forever.

Revelation 3:21 To him who overcomes I will grant to sit with Me on My throne, as I also overcame and sat down with My Father on His throne.

ADDITIONAL
RESOURCES

WHAT TO DO WHEN YOU
DON'T KNOW WHAT TO DO

In David Jeremiah's study on the book of James, we learn that a life devoted to God should impact the way we live day to day. Just like James, our doctrine should determine what we do and for whom we do it. This book can help us understand more clearly how to find God's strength in the midst of life's ups and downs so that we can walk the path of Christian maturity and live our lives for the One who made us.

Two great ways to order:

 800-947-1993 DavidJeremiah.org

Worry, loneliness, temptation, doubt—giants. We all have them; we all want to rid ourselves of them. But what does it look like to have a life free of these foes? In this book, Dr. David Jeremiah shares the key to slaying our daunting giants and gives us the tools we need to win the battle and live victoriously.

WHEN YOUR WORLD FALLS APART

Many of us have experienced life-threatening illness—or at least know someone who has. In *When Your World Falls Apart,* Dr. David Jeremiah shares his own battle against cancer as well as other real-life stories of people who have gone through similar trials. In addition, he highlights ten Psalms of encouragement to give hope to the moments that seem hopeless and light to our darkest days.

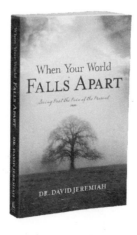

Two great ways to order:

 800-947-1993   DavidJeremiah.org

LIVING WITH CONFIDENCE
IN A CHAOTIC WORLD

Our world is filled with chaos. It is clear that we are living in the last days, but what are we to do until our final day here on earth? In this book, Dr. David Jeremiah identifies ten ways to live our days confidently in this world of uncertainty—staying compassionate toward others and staying connected to the Church, for example—all the while honoring Christ while doing so.

Two great ways to order:

About Dr. David Jeremiah

Dr. David Jeremiah is senior pastor of Shadow Mountain Community Church in El Cajon, California. He is the founder of *Turning Point*, a ministry committed to providing Christians with sound Bible teaching relevant to today's changing times through radio and television, the Internet, live events, and resource materials and books. A best-selling author, Dr. Jeremiah has written more than forty books including *Living with Confidence in a Chaotic World, What in the World Is Going On?, What Are You Afraid Of?* and *Agents of the Apocalypse*. He and his wife, Donna, have four grown children and twelve grandchildren.

TOPICAL INDEX

G

R

V

W

Notes

Notes

Notes

Notes

Notes

Notes

with Dr. David Jeremiah